ENDORSEMENTS

"*Millennial Orphan* is a shocking story of a young man's life from disaster to redemption. 'How can this be?' readers will ask after every overwhelming incident. 'Can these kinds of things actually happen to a child in our country?' Yes, they can. Thankfully, Jesus passionately seeks and completely saves the lost and Levi is a dynamic example that any life can be turned around through the intervention of the living God. That is the real story. No one continues to be an orphan when God's love enters the pilgrimage. What an encouragement this book is!"

TOM PHILLIPS, vice president
Billy Graham Evangelistic Association

"From the moment I picked up this book, I was completely mesmerized by *Millennial Orphan*. I figured I would read a chapter or two that first night, but instead I was up until dawn, often with tears in my eyes, unable to put it down. This story is powerful, it is relevant, and speaks to the deep pain felt by so many in this generation, but even louder it proclaims the love of a God that redeems all."

—JOSHUA CHARLES, www.thesacredhonor.com; coauthor of the #1 *New York Times* best seller *The Original Argument* with Glenn Beck

"Compelling. Raw. Honest. Empowering. Every couple of decades a book is published that speaks directly to the heart of a generation. *Millennial Orphan* will do for this generation what *The Cross and the Switchblade* did for a generation when it first appeared in the early 1960s. Levi's life story will shock you. From abuse to illness, from abandonment to gang violence, you'll find yourself saying, 'How can one person have experienced so much pain in the first twenty years of his life?' And then you'll find the answer—you, like Levi, can do all things through Christ who gives you strength. If you are looking for easy answers, this book is not for you. But if you are looking for real answers, hard-fought struggles with suffering and pain, hope that carries you through difficult times, then read this book. This book was written for you."

—PASTOR TOM STEPHEN, author of
Fearless: 40 Reflections on Fear

"An amazing story of perseverance, but also of being willing to listen when the truly important questions are spoken. Coworkers, friends, and even pastors fail us. But God doesn't. Levi tells that story."

—RICH BULLOCK, editor; author of the *Perilous Safety* series

"I have heard and read *a lot* of sad stories filled with pain and darkness. Stories that leave you emotionally doubled over. *Millennial Orphan* is different. It takes you on a journey. A journey that is sadly more common today for children than we'd like to admit. As Levi masterfully weaves his life story, he does so with tiny threads of hope and love. Those small but significant threads eventually allowed him to build a life that few believed he could fashion. Against all odds, evaluations, and poor prognosis, Levi did something unexpected … he lived. And better yet, *he conquered!*"

—GLENN GARVIN, director of National Camps
Royal Family Kids

"When I was asked to read and possibly endorse this book, I really didn't have the time to do so. However, once I began the book, I was instantly captured by the unfolding story. I became unable to hurry my way through. Levi Shepherd could have been and should have been no more than a statistic in many ways. However, he now stands a victorious warrior who is very clear on God's redemptive work in his life. The word 'miraculous' is often overused. However, not in this case. Levi's story is nothing short of a string of miracles woven through human tragedy. With every right to be bitter, callous, disillusioned, and angry, Levi emerges as a strong, God-praising victor. This book has instantly made it on my 'pass out to friends list.'"

—ALAN SMYTH, regional director of
Greater Los Angeles Young Life (www.younglife.org)
author of *Prized Possession*; www.myfatherdaughter.com

"Even at a young age, Levi discovered that 'life was dangerous territory.' Pain, abandonment, illness, betrayal, and disappointment left holes in his soul. But amidst the darkness, he discovered light, healing, companionship, hope, and faith. Against all odds, he conquered.

Not through a formula or pious behavior, but by listening, waiting, submitting, and yielding.

Levi's journey isn't a simple quest; it's more of a perplexing detour; with long periods of feeling lost. It's messy—like real life."

—TIMOTHY SMITH, family coach and
author of *The Danger of Raising Nice Kids;* www.ParentsCoach.org

"If you want to read a book that exemplifies the redemptive power of Christ when it seems like all the odds are stacked against you, this is your book. It is unbelievable what Levi fought through by the grace of God to even be alive today to write his testimony. *Millennial Orphan* is the ultimate comeback story."

—CRAIG JOHNSON, author of *Lead Vertically,*
director of ministry, Lakewood Church

"Compelling, inspiring, and an easy read. What an incredibly difficult childhood through young adulthood. And, yet, what an amazing story of God's power and compassion. Working in a busy urban trauma center, I often see the tragic results of childhood illness, child abuse, and gang violence, and somehow through God's grace, Levi survived all of these and more. This is a book that I would recommend to anyone who is struggling and questioning why God is allowing tragedies in their life."

—DR. MICHAEL STEPHEN, MD
St. Francis Hospital, Los Angeles, CA

"*Millennial Orphan* is a touching story that will move you in so many ways. Whether you are working with someone who has come from a difficult place, or have walked a similar road yourself, this book will remind you that God can be pursuing you, even when you are totally unaware of what is really going on. And it is a story that will give you valuable insights into the life experience and perspective of someone who has been in foster care."

—JOHN FRANKLIN, executive director, Dark to Dawn

"It is with joy that I encourage you to read *Millennial Orphan*. I have known Levi like a son for the past seven years, and I have watched his journey along the road of healing and redemption from devastating circumstance and the uncontrollable decisions of others. I have seen Levi scale the daunting mountains of his own hurt and his own pride. With Levi it has not always been pretty, but it has been genuine—it has been real. Levi bears the marks of his struggles, on his body and in his soul. And due to the intense struggles he has walked through in his life, Levi has a keen awareness to what God is speaking to him and teaching him—even when he doesn't want to be taught. *Millennial Orphan* puts in perspective suffering and victory, setbacks and advances, defeat and what it is to be a conqueror. By reading this story, you will understand a bit more the loving heart of God. It isn't always easy, this walk with the Lord, but it is always worth it."

—STEVE SIPP, pastor, House to House Ministries

"I met Levi six years ago through a string of people and phone calls. He was a stranger, but a *brother* in need of a roof over his head, encouragement, and true fellowship. Having been there myself, I found it impossible to say no, and invited him to come call my couch his own, not knowing that I would be blessed, as well, with one of the most edifying friendships I have known.

Levi has become a brother to me, and I have found that in my times of need he is there to challenge, encourage, and bless me. His heart and passion for the Lord is deep and sincere. Levi has abandoned his life in search of truth and a life of humility.

His faith has been tested through great struggles, but has birthed into a source of inspiration and hope, sharpening others along with me. No matter what comes his way, Levi stands firmly in faith, while being anchored in the hope he has in our Messiah.

Levi's story is a unique and moving example of the trials that we face in our lives, but a testimony of power, power that comes *only* through being fully surrendered to the Lord.

Millennial Orphan has the power to convict, uplift, and strengthen us all in times of adversity."

—SEAN ELLSWORTH, friend of the author

MILLENNIAL ORPHAN

TRUST YOUR STRUGGLE.
GOD IS STRONGER.

LEVI GIDEON SHEPHERD

BroadStreet
PUBLISHING

Published by BroadStreet Publishing Group, LLC
Racine, Wisconsin, USA
BroadStreetPublishing.com

Millennial Orphan
Trust Your Struggle. God Is Stronger.

Cover design by Chris Garborg at garborgdesign.com
Interior by Katherine Lloyd at theDESKonline.com

Printed in the United States of America
16 17 18 19 20 5 4 3 2 1

This book is dedicated to
the loving memory of my mother.

Mom, there is not a day that goes by that I don't
think of you. We didn't have long together, but you
laid a foundation that has let me grow into the man
I am today, and I hope that man would make
you proud. I love and miss you dearly.

WHY I WROTE
MILLENNIAL ORPHAN

A few years back, friends and acquaintances began to encourage me to tell my story. In time their encouragement grew to a shout, and one day I gave in.

We live in a cynical, fallen world—one which is ever increasingly falling to pieces, and if I could do only one thing, say one thing, to help a hurting soul it would be this:

God is bigger than the struggle—the struggles of our life and the pain we feel. He longs to meet us in them, to prove himself. To prove he is love and to give us hope.

This is my story of just that.

CONTENTS

FOREWORD

"You don't know me, but my name is Levi Shepherd, and I'm good friends with…"

That's the first thing I heard when I answered a call on my mobile phone while waiting in the drive-thru at McDonald's. By the time I got to the window to pay for ice cream cones for my three kids, I had agreed to read Levi's book and give him feedback. When I got home, a *very* rough draft of the book was waiting in my e-mail inbox.

Levi's energy, passion, and his humble-yet-in-your-face approach to a complete stranger intrigued me. I liked him almost instantly, and I would soon discover why.

I printed off the draft of *Millennial Orphan* and had a tough time putting it down. Levi's life story grabbed me immediately. Here was a man who discovered the truth that in Christ we can overcome anything.

And Levi has had a lot to overcome: poverty; sexual abuse by a church member; cancer; an absent father; a mom who died young; the foster-care system; gang culture; drug abuse; emotional isolation; a failed parachute deployment on an army training jump; and the list continues.

As I read, I was overwhelmed by the amount of tragedy Levi experienced in his young life. I longed for his relief—and then it happened. God stepped in, and Levi found the possibility of hope, love, and purpose. And what I have seen since Levi first released his book is that others who have experienced abuse, abandonment, profound disappointments, the foster-care system, and gang life have found the same hope—the same God who encounters us in the midst of our struggles. Readers have related both to Levi's discouragement and his desire for a God who meets us in the darkest times.

Levi's voice and book speaks to a generation who has lost hope in God. And he speaks to all those who have become disillusioned with a Christianity that seems powerless to confront real questions and deep hurts.

Our initial conversation in the McDonald's drive-thru developed into a friendship with Levi. As he and I have talked, I've seen him live out his contentious relationship with God. I've experienced his profound love for and frustration with God.

As I read about God's faithfulness in Levi's life, I felt both encouraged and empowered to walk through the difficult and challenging issues in my life.

My prayer is this: No matter what you face, whether it's the same struggles Levi has endured or something completely different, that you will look up and see God, that he is there, willing and ready to meet your every need. That's what this book is about.

Levi and I have talked and encouraged each other a lot over the past couple of years. I've seen him at the point of total discouragement even while writing about a God who had encouraged him his whole life. That's what I love about Levi: he's honest and he's raw. This is also what I love about our God—God is both honest and raw. When we bring our honest selves to God, warts and all, God brings healing and hope.

May the Lord bless you in huge ways as you read *Millennial Orphan*!

—TOM STEPHEN, author of *Fearless: 40 Reflections on Fear*
senior pastor, Monte Vista Presbyterian Church

To the one who conquers I will give a place to sit with me on my throne, just as I have conquered and have sat down with my Father on his throne.

—Revelation 3:21 ISV

1

SHADOWBOXING

I was the surprise gift of a one-night stand.

In 1983, early on a snowy December afternoon in Kansas City, Missouri, my mother, Lynn, gave birth to me at Truman Medical Center, located on the edge of the inner city.

My father had taken off shortly after I was conceived, so Mom raised my older sister, Misty, and me on her own, trying to make ends meet with welfare and whatever work hours she could get at the gas station down the road.

We lived in a duplex in the ghetto, where the sounds of police sirens serenaded the nights, and boarded-up businesses accented with the latest graffiti guarded the gateways of our community. This was our home, a drug- and crime-filled neighborhood where we, as Caucasians, were the minority.

My mother had two failed marriages before my birth, and my sister and I had different fathers. Mom was constantly in and out of relationships, and I, as an innocent three-year-old, wondered if any of the revolving carousels of men was my father. I was let down time and again when I found they were not.

This was my life—not pretty, but also not unlike that of so many in our neighborhood. I didn't realize it at the time, but life was shaping me even then.

We left the rough part of East Kansas City because Mom needed to escape a bad relationship. Her boyfriend was a drug addict who would often come to our house just to beat my mother or use her for his own selfish physical needs. Though Mom did her best to shield Misty and me when he was on a terror, we still noticed the aftermath:

the split lip, the purple bruises, the arm cradled to her side. I think that changed me inside, hardened me a little to the world around us.

We moved only a short distance to nearby Independence, trading one rough part of town for another, and settled into another duplex. My great-uncle Vince ran an inner-city establishment there called the Whatsoever Community Center, and not long after our move, Vince offered Mom a job as his assistant at the center.

This was exactly what she needed: a steady job with great pay and benefits that could help her raise my sister and me in a safer environment. The money even allowed Mom to go back to school part time. On the days she worked at the center, Uncle Vince agreed I could tag along, sort of paid day care. The center is where I spent most of my time from age three to eight.

Whatsoever became a second home, and as a young child, there was much to take in. The center helped many Kansas City area kids and families, but to me the most interesting program was its training gym for local boxers.

Young and fatherless, I became fascinated with these men who came to train at the gym day in and day out. Every spare moment, I slipped away from my mother's side and sneaked through the corridors down to the east-wing basement where the gym was located.

From a concealed corner, breathing in the sweaty, stale air, I watched the boxers work as the trainers shouted commands. They jumped rope, lifted weights, and pounded away at the punching bags hung along the wall. In my young mind, I thought they were superheroes.

I was even more convinced of their special powers when they stepped into the ring and sparred with each other. Powerful punches sent a distinctive *whomp* echoing throughout the gym. But to my surprise, each blow left the men unfazed, and they just went on sparring.

They have to be superheroes, I thought to myself. They aren't getting hurt from the wallops. Before this, my only experience with violence was watching my mother apply another coat of foundation to hide the wounds inflicted by her boyfriend. When she was struck, she got hurt. Not these guys. I shadowboxed in the dim light, feinting with my left fist, then delivering a knockout punch with my right.

Too soon, my mother would come looking for me.

"Levi," she'd call through the door of the gym. "Come on, honey. It's time to come back upstairs." She always played along, as if she had just realized I was gone, when in reality I'd been in the corner of that gym for hours each time I snuck away.

That was my mom, always letting me wander to the places my heart longed to be. She'd been thirty-two years old when I was born. With her golden blonde hair falling to her waist, I always thought she was an angel. I'm not sure why my mother seldom smiled—most likely it was due to the strain of life; hard work had been the only way of life she had ever known. I remember how calloused her hands felt and the soothing comfort of her sky-blue eyes.

To the rest of the world, she was a gorgeous woman who had made more than her share of bad decisions. To our little family, she was our rock. She worked hard to provide a safe life for my sister and me. In my eyes, Mom was precious beyond words. I might have been the man of the house by default, but I was still my mama's baby boy through and through.

As the months passed, we became more and more involved at the center. Mom would often get there at dawn and stay late into the evening. She was gifted at almost anything she put her mind to but was especially talented in the kitchen, where she could cook beyond our taste buds' wildest dreams.

Whatsoever partnered with the United Way several times each year for all-you-can-eat spaghetti dinners to raise funds for the United Way's programs. As part of the outreach, major league players from both the Kansas City Royals and Chiefs would participate.

As most little boys do, I daydreamed about being one of them when I grew up, and they quickly became my childhood heroes. I still remember how they would come up to my mother long after the banquets had ended and ask if they could take home some of her spaghetti. Just as they left an impression with me, so had my mother's spaghetti impressed them!

Those were great times. But life is forever changing, and it was about to add another interesting wrinkle.

Stephen, my birth father, was a tall, charming, handsome man, with dark hair, brown eyes, and tattoos all over. As a young man, he had served as a gunner on a navy riverboat on Vietnam's Mekong Delta. When he was "in country," their swift boat crew's sole job was to escort a small team of commandos (Navy SEALs or a Ranger Long Range Reconnaissance Patrol) up the Mekong to their next mission. These daily trips steaming upriver to their next firefight, outnumbered and outgunned, changed him inside. Some of those memories he would recount to me later in one of his drunken stupors. The things he saw would make the most valiant of men break down and cry. Without regard for the unnerving danger they knew lay ahead of them, they carried on with their mission, just like the rest of our brave veterans.

The things my father witnessed and did with his own hands left him with a thousand-yard stare, a forever distant gaze, as if some part of him—a part he desperately needed—had been marooned on those faraway muddy river banks. For my father's heroism in the war, he was awarded the Navy Cross, our nation's second-highest combat decoration. But medals can never make up for what a man forfeits of his soul.

After three tours of duty, his days in the navy ended. So had the war. And while he had been a courageous soldier, when it came to being my father, he was missing in action. Inevitably, his personal pain found its way into our relationship.

My memories of him during my early years included him coming around in the middle of the night, banging on our front door. He'd prop himself up against the wall to keep from falling over in his drunken stupor and yell for my mother to take him back. The pleading message was always the same, as if her presence would soothe his heartache. She always sent him away as quickly as he appeared, often reminding him as he went that he had yet to pay a dime in child support, and that he wasn't welcome into our life until he cleaned up his act.

He'd vanish back into the night, just like the enemies he fought in Vietnam. My father had always lived by his own terms and was not one to be told what to do, and we wouldn't hear from him until the next time of *his* choosing.

Several times a year—besides the nighttime visits—there were signs that my father had resurfaced. We'd find a gift for me on our front porch, along with a pile of crushed cigarette butts. Maybe he didn't know when my birthday was, or maybe he was just too drunk to remember. Regardless, the gifts were never around the right date. My mother would come to me with the packages, asking if I wanted to keep them, and every time I declined. My heart just wasn't able to receive something from a man who scared the daylights out of me.

***

By the time I was four, my mother had started taking my sister and me to a little Methodist church down the street from my grandfather Harold's house. My grandfather (my mother's stepfather, actually) was an usher at the church, and he also helped with odd jobs around the building. The church was an old cobblestone structure, with several varying levels that sprawled over the property—like many of the traditional churches scattered throughout America.

It wasn't too long before my mother began leading Sunday school for the preschoolers. Some of my initial memories of God and church are of my mother talking about God while using flannel figures of Jesus, his disciples, and animals.

We had only been involved with the church for a brief time when one day I was sitting in my Sunday school class and had to use the bathroom. I wasn't in my mother's class and had another teacher. I began waving my hand back and forth fiercely like all little kids do when they "urgently" need something. After a brief moment, the teacher acknowledged me with a scowl and dismissed herself from the class as she led me out of the room. We arrived at the boys' room, and she directed me into the stall. I finished my business and attempted to leave the stall, only to be blocked by the teacher stepping into it. She locked the door behind her. Confused, I tried to push past her and get out. She then grabbed me and told me to do things that are unworthy of retelling here. Alone and trapped with her, my teacher took away my childhood innocence. When it was over, she scolded, "You won't tell anyone about this, or you will make God very angry with you!"

I was too young to realize the ugliness of her lies. I was convinced this God was a mean, mean man.

Stephen continued to make appearances during this time. You could not have guessed by his actions, but he had a very good-paying job as a foreman at Grainger, one of the largest warehouses in the country. My dad hired one of the best family law attorneys he could find and took my mom to court for custodial rights.

The court ordered my mother to take me to see a family counselor so they could determine which parent I wanted to live with. Each time we went, my mother would entrust me to the counselor, who guided me into her office to meet with me alone. When I asked the counselor if she wanted me to "do" with her what my Sunday school teacher made me do, the counselor realized the teacher was molesting me. As you can imagine, this unleashed chaos in the church we attended. The Sunday school teacher was asked to leave the church and was arrested. But she wasn't the only person to leave the church due to that controversy.

The court awarded my father provisional custody, allowing him to take me on supervised visits twice each month. After six months of supervised visits, he was allowed to have them unsupervised. I didn't welcome this, but no one in the courts seemed to really care what *my* wishes were. Visitation with my dad was the biggest change of my young life.

As a child, everything going on was out of my control, yet all of it powerfully influenced every facet of who I was, from how I saw the world to how, and whom, I trusted. Life became dangerous territory.

However, through all this, God still had me in the palm of his hand—though I did not know him at the time. What I *did* know of God were lies I received from a disturbed Sunday school teacher. I suppose it's fitting that, at the time all of this was going on, my favorite song was one my mother had taught me: "He's Got the Whole World in His Hands." God was there with me, and nothing was going to change that—not even my father.

I found it impossible to call him Dad, opting instead to call him by his first name, Stephen.

Most of the time he wouldn't refer to me by my first name; to him I was his "little buddy," and he always treated me more like a friend than his son. Maybe he was scared by the fact that I was *his* responsibility.

He did do his best to take me out to do things that fathers do with their sons. On nice days we would go fly a kite in the park, or I would hold tight to the playground swing and squeal with terror and delight as he pushed me high into the air.

Our most memorable custody visit we had together was a trip to see the Blue Angels Air Show that had come to town. It was one of those hot, dreadfully humid summer days that Missouri does so well, and the crowd was so heavy that I had to sit on my dad's shoulders. Hesitantly I clasped his hands to stay balanced, as sweat soaked both of us where our bodies touched.

"Look, Levi!" My dad pointed up into the distance. An iconic blue F-18 came screeching across the sky and banked sharply. The pilot buried the throttle, and the plane roared skyward. I let go of my father and clasped my hands over my ears, watching the plane disappear into dark thunderclouds forming above.

A few more aerial acts performed before a strong rain with a growling thunder forced our crowd into several hangers where souvenirs and keepsakes were sold. Rain rattled symphonically against the steel structure while a welcomed wet breeze helped cool the stifling air inside.

Only the grand finale remained, and once the storm passed a voice came over the PA system telling us we could all return to the viewing area.

"This is something we don't want to miss!" my dad said. We climbed onto some bleachers as a large, dark plane, much bigger than all the planes we had seen that day, broke from the foggy clouds high above. Then I saw them. First one, then a second, and within minutes, dozens of parachutes filled the sky.

"Are those men flying?" I asked my dad from atop my perch.

He laughed. "Sure are! Those are paratroopers—some of the bravest soldiers around."

My eyes filled with delight as I watched those men fall from the sky.

A paratrooper. I was sold. When I grew up, I wanted to be a paratrooper!

Stephen took me back to his house after the show to go swimming in his backyard pool. I hadn't learned to swim, so he sat me on his back as he swam from one end of the pool to the next. Frightened by being in a large pool for the first time—and having to cling to a man that I was still hesitant about—at one point I hopped off his back and lunged for the side. Not having the strength to make the distance, I quickly sank in the deep water. The seconds I spent submerged seemed like an eternity, though Stephen immediately snatched me out of the water and hoisted me onto the deck. He was enraged and cursed at me while I sat shivering in a towel on one of the deck chairs, too afraid to cry.

He grabbed up my clothes, tossed me into his car, and slammed the door. Within minutes we arrived at my house and he ran to the door. Still steaming with anger, he mashed the doorbell over and over, as if the annoyance would force my mother to respond faster. When Mom opened the door, Stephen gave her an earful about how much of a "wuss" her son was. He said I never was his son in the first place, only hers!

My mother, though short and graciously beautiful, could more than hold her own in a confrontation. She lit into Stephen, chewing him up one side and down the other, as she strode toward his car to retrieve me. As she and I retreated to the porch, my dad peeled away in his souped-up Mustang, tires screeching in a childish tantrum. With him there were no good-byes, and this was the last time I'd see my dad for quite some time.

<hr />

We grow up in a fallen and cold world. As kids we're powerless, at the mercy of those around us, including our parents. We cannot change who our parents are or how they choose to raise us. One thing I've learned is they are just human, and they must account for their lives just as we do today.

At that time, there was only one person I trusted, and that was my mom. Was she perfect? No, but I didn't know that, and I adored her. Even with all the turmoil around us, she did her best to raise my sister and me with good values and hope. At least she *tried* to point me to the One who could give me hope.

In our house, especially my bedroom, she'd hang pictures of Jesus—someone she called God. He had long hair, a pale complexion, and a beard to boot. I didn't like those pictures because the man I saw resembled many of the men my mother had brought into our lives, and that was not a compliment. I was scared of him, so I'd often take the pictures down. I got in trouble for that, and my mother would hang them back up, admonishing me to stop being "irreverent."

There was one picture of Jesus I didn't take down. It happened to be the one she had hung above my bed. Something about that picture captivated me. Jesus stood knocking on a door in the middle of the night—just like my father did sometimes. Unlike the other pictures, this one didn't scare me. There was something about the way light radiated from Jesus, illuminating the door. A peaceful expression on his face mesmerized me. The picture left me with lingering questions: Where was the doorknob? Why was it the middle of the night?

At some point, my mother's routine of rehanging the photos came about, and I stopped her mid-act to ask about the picture.

She paused and stared at the painting for a moment before she said, "Levi, he stands outside the door because he wants to come in and be with you."

"Why?" I asked in innocence.

"Because he loves you!"

"He's a stranger! How can he love me? Why? It's the middle of the night; isn't he scared of the dark?"

My mother chuckled, putting her arm around me in a hug. "Honey, God will only be a stranger to you if you don't let him in. And he is never afraid of the dark."

Leaning down, my mother kissed my forehead. "He's not like other men. He is never going to leave you, even if he has to stand there until you let him in. Levi, he will never leave you."

Such simple words: *He is not like other men.* What did she mean by that? She was always so straightforward with me, yet this time she left me with more questions than answers. God was a stranger, at least in my eyes, and yet he loved me and was never going to leave me?

Maybe I would have been more comforted by my mother's words if I'd known the coming reality. Life was about to get far more ugly than anything my family had known to this point—especially for me.

2

FIRE IN MY BONES

Four years old. Something is wrong. *Drastically* wrong! I woke up screaming in the middle of the night.

"*Mommy, mommy!* My bones are on fire!" Doubled over, I clutched at my thighs, trying to smother the burning pain deep inside.

Mom flipped on the light as she ran into the room. She had just made it to the bed when a hot stream of vomit spewed from my mouth onto both of us. Not deterred, she scooped me in her arms and held me as I shivered. Immediately another round of vomit came. Oh, did it come.

Her cheeks dripped as she rocked me in her arms. "Please ... Jesus ... please ... Lord," she quietly prayed out loud.

When the sudden chaos calmed, my mother carried me across the hall to the bedroom she shared with my sister.

"Misty, please get up. We're going to the hospital."

After hours of waiting in the lobby, one of the doctors examined me. My mother was told that everything was okay, that it was likely a virus and could be taken care of with some ibuprofen and rest. I wish it had been that simple.

The night episodes continued with increasing intensity. Desperate for answers, my mother began taking me to any doctor with whom she could get an appointment. Each exam left only questions, as no one could find the reason for my ailment. Finally, I was admitted to the hospital for observation to see if my illness could be seen in action. It struck with dependable frequency.

Like the times before, I woke up screaming for my mother as I clutched at my legs and vomited in my bed. Only this time I wasn't in *my* bed; I was in the hospital. Mom had been keeping watch over me. She ran into the hallway and yelled for the nurse. One rushed into the room and saw what had grown to be the familiar sight for my family:

a four-year-old boy doubled over in feverish sweat, shivering in a pool of his own vomit, and crying from the pain.

"I think we need to get him to Children's Mercy," the nurse said as she helped my mom clean me up.

The next day, I was transferred to Children's Mercy, the local children's hospital, where I underwent countless medical tests while the staff continued observation. A brief stay followed before we were sent home to await the results of my tests.

⚬⚬⚬

On my mother's thirty-sixth birthday, my grandparents came over to celebrate with a summer cookout. A thick charcoal smoke from the grill rolled through our backyard. As the phone rang, Mom handed my grandma the tongs to the grill and ran inside the house.

Quite a bit of time passed, then my mother called out through the kitchen window, "Levi, honey, come here."

I stopped my game of whiffle ball with Grandpa and ran inside.

My mother sat at the kitchen table. Streaks of makeup ran down her cheeks, a mountain of wadded tissues sat by one hand. Mom had always been the strong one in our family, and I had seldom seen her cry.

She scooped me up in the strongest hug known to man, though even that couldn't remove the tension inside the room.

"Levi, I got a call from the doctors," she whispered softly as she leaned down and kissed my cheek. "There is a war going on in your body, one that the good guys aren't winning."

She paused, gazing into my eyes, squeezing me even tighter. "There are some things we have to go through. Where you'll have to be very, very brave; but I know you can do it, because you're Mommy's boy!"

She brushed her eyes dry and smiled, even though she didn't look happy. My stomach tensed at her words. I didn't have the slightest clue what she meant, but it scared me that a woman who was always so full of peace and comfort was shaken by something she could not change. And whatever it was, was inside of me.

"You know how you love to play war with your army men in

Mommy's garden? I need you to play army. This time, instead of playing out in the yard, let's pretend that the army men are inside your body fighting the bad guys. Can you do that for Mommy?"

"You mean like fighting the brown army, but in my body?" A smiled formed across my face—I *loved* to play army!

"Yes, you can fight the brown army in your body."

Only the war I would fight was not one of make-believe, the way I tried to vanquish an enemy with some funny childhood name in tiny hand-dug trenches along the carrots and green beans in our backyard garden. It was a battle to be fought in the marrow of my bones, and it *did* have a name, a very ugly one—*cancer*.

⸻

Our small, close-knit family, my grandparents, and my aunt and uncle gathered in a small waiting room in the oncology unit at Children's Mercy. Shortly thereafter, the pastor from the church joined us, and my mother fell into his arms in a brief moment of vulnerable grief.

A nurse came calling for me at the edge of the lobby, and Mom looked around the room to each family member. Words were no comfort in times like this, and their faces said it all.

She knelt down and looked into my eyes. Her chin quivered as she ran her hand through my hair. Not for a moment did her gaze leave mine. Quietly, her words came to my ears as she whispered, "I love you."

A mother's instinct is to bear all she can for her child, and I know, if given the chance, my mom would have carried this burden too. But this was beyond her control.

Even if she couldn't carry this *for* me, she could carry *me*. She scooped me up and followed behind the nurse, holding me tightly in one arm as she gripped our pastor with the other.

The nurse guided us to a treatment room barely big enough for four people. In the center was a table, and beside it was a surgical tray holding several vials, needles, and syringes, all neatly arranged in their sterile packaging.

A handsome black man, outfitted in green scrubs, stood at a sink in the corner. "I'm Dr. Woods, it's so nice to meet you." He walked over and hugged both of us, me sandwiched in between. "I know that we can never really be ready for something like this," he said to my mother.

As the doctor went back to washing his hands, another nurse squeezed into the room and handed my mother a cartoon-printed hospital gown. Mom hoisted me up on the table and began helping me change out of my clothes.

I began to shake as terror overwhelmed me.

"Mommy … I want to go home. I don't like this place."

My mother cradled my cheeks with her palms and leaned forward to kiss my forehead.

"We can't, honey. We can't." She clutched me tightly in her arms.

No one had to tell me that I wasn't going to like whatever was about to happen.

"Remember how I said yesterday I needed you to be really brave for Mommy?" she continued. "This is one of those times I need you to be really brave, and you are brave, sweetie! We can do this—together. I promise. Mommy isn't going to leave your side. I will be right here, always!"

I clung to my mother's hands while I listened, never taking my eyes off her. Mom spoke of a war I was losing, one aiming to end my life. Now was the time to fight back. Today was the day I would begin chemotherapy.

"Levi, can you lie down for me, son?" Dr. Woods asked as he came up alongside the table.

Still a shaking mess, I leaned back to the table as Dr. Woods helped guide me into the fetal position on my side. The nurse positioned herself in front of me to hold me still, blocking my view of Mom. I shot from the table.

"Mommy … Mommy!" I shouted, trying to fight my way back to her.

"Honey, I'm right here. I'm not going anywhere. I'm right here!" she said. Unable to get to me, she took her long, waist-length blonde hair, draped it across the nurse's arm, and let it fall right in my face. I grabbed the makeshift security blanket—a sign of her never-changing presence—and held on for dear life.

"Here we go, Levi," Dr. Woods said. I felt his gloved hand run along the small of my back. He cleaned a small spot with disinfectant. "You are going to feel a small, loud-sounding bee sting here where my hand is, but I need you to hold as still as you can for me until I'm done, okay? Can you do that for me?"

The nurse in front of me rubbed my arms comfortingly as he spoke, and she forced a smile.

"Yes … I c-c-caan," my lips fumbled for words.

Milliseconds after I assured him I would hold still, *snaaap!*

The medical gun holding the first vial pierced into my spine and began delivering chemotherapy intrathecally into my nervous system.

My wail no doubt carried down the hallway. Dr. Woods had lied to me. It was far more than a bee sting. It was a day that no child or adult should have to live through, and it was just the first of many. Yet living was the whole point, and the pain was necessary to win the war.

Dr. Woods finished the spinal tap and performed a bone marrow aspiration to test the exact count of lymphatic cancer cells in my blood.

Chemotherapy—only a handful of years old at the time—was just now being used on kids. Not sure of the proper dosages for tiny bodies, physicians bombed away with it. Today, only a fraction of chemo is used compared to what they gave children back then.

The admonition to be a brave little soldier was, well, an understatement at the very least. I wasn't even five years old, and I was already facing something that threatened to wipe me off the face of the earth. On top of that, I routinely received spinal taps with chemo and steroids, pills, and intravenous injections that left my little world spinning. And I lost my hair.

The doctors gave me (and the other kids undergoing the same treatment) only a 20 percent chance of survival. For every ten kids who were diagnosed with cancer back then, only two lived. I was one of the two.

⸎

Could I blame God for what happened to me? I could try, I guess, but the argument doesn't stand up. This isn't what he had in mind when he created all that there is—heaven and earth. He created us to walk with him in *life* and gave us the priceless gift of free will to do so.

But we chose what *we* wanted, and ever since, death is what we know. We will all be born. And we will all die. Everyone knows this, and we can't escape it. But will we truly *live* with the time we are given?

God is resoundingly sovereign! Was the cancer in my body going to change this? *No!* He was still fully in control. After all, he is God. No matter what I believed or didn't believe about him at the time, that would not change. And just as my mother echoed to me as a child, he was never going to leave me.

As life played out, I was going to see how true this was. He was with me, in control, despite everything that would happen.

3

HERE TODAY AND GONE TOMORROW

During 1987, any time I wasn't at Children's Mercy I was at home, trying to experience a little bit of normalcy. Due to regular chemotherapy treatments, I couldn't participate in activities other kids my age could, and that included school.

I was homeschooled from kindergarten to the second grade. So, apart from the other children at the hospital, I was somewhat isolated from other kids. And my chemo-induced bald head and puffy complexion didn't help. My family became my world, and they came through for me.

Aunt Tracy, my mother's sister, was a huge bright spot in the dreariness of those days. She was the first to hold me when I'd been born, so we shared a special bond throughout my young life.

Tracy was an equity partner at a local law firm in the metro area. Having never married and in her early forties, she became the best friend I could have during my cancer years. She would come over and take me out to do fun things: evenings on a lake as we cast fishing lures into the water, or a night at the ballpark for a Royals game.

She also found a special way to embolden my spirits as I went forward with my treatment. Being well established in her profession, and with no family of her own to support, she decided to give me a bonus of one hundred dollars for every spinal tap I endured. At my age, I couldn't even count that high yet, but I knew a hundred dollars bought a lot of Legos. By the time I went through fifteen spinal tap treatments, I had a Lego stash that filled several toy totes. Tracy's reward and her love helped pull me through those difficult days, and I'll never forget that.

Somehow there was a peace surrounding me, a calm, and it allowed me to survive those terrible yet necessary treatments. And that peace certainly didn't come from inside me!

One day, not long into my treatment at Children's Mercy, Dr. Woods came to my mother and shared that the staff had noticed there was a hope about me, one he wished some of the other kids could experience. At his request, my mother asked me if I'd be willing to go play in the rooms with other boys and girls who "need a loving friend to play with them." What I didn't know was that these kids, my new friends, were on the verge of losing their fights with cancer.

Who knew that something so simple as playing a video game, opening a new toy, or sharing a laugh could help save someone's life by giving them something to look forward to? But ask any cancer survivor and they will tell you *hope* is the difference between life and death.

The harsh reality for me was that lots of hope didn't always overcome cancer. One day I would be playing with a boy or a girl and hug them good-bye with the promise I'd see them in a few days. I'd come back to the hospital and find they were no longer there. At first, I was told they'd gone "home." But I quickly figured out the harsh reality of that statement. Life had barely begun for them—a few years—and now it was over.

⚮

One day during one of my countless inpatient visits, my mother and I left my room and made a break for the cafeteria. As we rode down on the elevator—with one of her hands holding mine, and the other steadying the rolling IV stand—the car stopped en route to the ground floor, and the doors opened on a familiar face. It was Dusty's mom. Dusty and I had become good friends at the hospital, and I played with him often. Dusty and his mom were inseparable, just like my mom and me. Only this time he wasn't by her side.

Dusty's mom silently entered the elevator. Her eyes were bloodshot, and black streaks of mascara ran down her face. As soon as the doors closed, my mom wrapped her arms around Dusty's mom. They both just cried in each other's embrace. Nothing needed to be said. At twelve years old, Dusty had lost his life to cancer.

When the ding announced our arrival at the main floor, Dusty's mom mumbled a thank-you and left the elevator. When she was out of sight, Mom knelt beside me and hugged me.

"I love you so much, Levi!" she whispered, as she held on to me tightly. "Mommy is so proud of you."

⤚⤙⤚

Not long after Dusty's death, I was again going through one of my inpatient visits and happened to share a room with a young boy who had been left there all alone. No mother. No father. No other family. He was *alone*, and this greatly bothered me. Unless she stepped out for a smoke break, or went down to the cafeteria for a reprieve from the monotonous meals brought to us, my mom was *always* there.

The boy often cried out for his mommy, but she never came. For most of the day he cried, and sometimes his bouts would leave him choking for air. His only company was the nurses who came with their needles and their pain.

That evening my mother left for a while and returned later with a box that every young person covets: a Happy Meal. With a kiss on top of my head, she plopped the treasure down before me on the hospital tray and said she'd be right back. That meant she was going for a cigarette. As soon as she left, I tore open the box and dove in for my toy.

But I was caught off guard by silence in the room. Though he usually cried nonstop, my roommate was now silent. A whispered, "Oh!" echoed in the air.

I turned, and he was sitting in his bed, his cheeks streaked and his thumb in his mouth. His eyes were wide with delight as he stared at my Happy Meal. He too knew awesomeness hid inside.

Moved by the sight, I got out of my bed, wheeled my tray with me, and climbed onto his bed with my meal.

"Here, we can share," I said, as I divided the chicken nuggets and fries onto the blanket. "You can have the toy, too, if you like."

The young boy smiled from ear to ear, an adorable grin that left his cheeks pocketed with two dimples as he reached for the toy. For a few moments we sat there together, eating our fries and playing with the toy car, but then we were abruptly interrupted by a nurse who came to change his catheter.

We were in trouble. Well, I was in trouble. She scolded me and shooed me back to my own bed, then took away the remaining meal from my friend. My mom returned right then, and the nurse gave her the food—along with a lecture that we not share our food with the boy since he was unable to have anything solid for now.

I just sat there quietly as the nurse berated my mom, while in the bed beyond the two talking women, the boy smiled as he raced the car along his legs. "*Vroom … vrrrooom.*"

It was peaceful the rest of the evening. A smile on his face until we all fell asleep for the night.

The next morning we woke to a frenzy of nurses rushing into our room and tearing past the privacy curtain. The boy in the next bed lay motionless as several nurses began mouth-to-mouth resuscitation. After several minutes and no response, a doctor came in and drew the sheet up over his head. Then they wheeled him out of the room. His heart had stopped. Just like that, my friend was gone.

It wasn't long until I had my own brush with death.

⁓

By the time I was six years old, the cancer had taken a bad turn. I was no longer responding to the chemotherapy. Things got dramatically worse when I was hospitalized with pneumonia.

My doctors frantically worked to boost my platelet count. They planned a blood transfusion and then a new brand of chemotherapy. But I was so sick and weak that my veins would roll and collapse every time they tried to insert an IV line.

The hospital staff moved me to a triage room where several nurses took turns attempting to place an IV line into my frail arms. Each time, the vein would roll, and roll again, then collapse. They eventually went to my legs but had the same results.

This dragged on for hours. Thankfully, between each salvo of needle sticks, they let me rest on the triage room table under a pile of warmed, bleach-scented hospital blankets, shivering from a combination of fever and pain from all the failed attempts to place a line.

My mother, not allowed in the room even when I was resting, sat in the observation room. I could see her through the window and hear her muffled phone conversation.

"Please hurry. This could be it … you need to come quick. This could be it." She choked back a sob and mopped her face with shredded tissues.

As the night drew on, I grew weaker. My threshold for pain had long since passed, and I was somewhat numb as I lay dozing on the table. When awake, I was nearly blinded by the brilliant triage lights above, but I also saw that my family had all gathered in the observation room. Every few minutes, the nurse beside me would assure me that I was going to be okay. Tired and weak, I gave in to the weight of my eyelids and closed my eyes.

Meanwhile, in a desperate search for anyone who could help, Children's Mercy located a gifted doctor in St. Louis who had the reputation as one who could place an IV line into any vein no matter how fiercely it rolled or threatened to collapse. Dr. Mary agreed to come and boarded a helicopter for her flight to Kansas City.

A team of nurses met Dr. Mary at the helipad and escorted her to my room. With the grace of a saint, she lifted the mountain of blankets that kept me warm and leaned down to kiss my forehead.

"Levi … sweetie, can you open your eyes for me?"

Groggily, as if sedated, I forced my eyes open and strained to focus past the surgical light above and onto the figure that hovered over me.

"Are you … an angel?" I asked, barely able to get the words out of my parched throat. She had snow-white hair, radiant blue eyes, and skin that glowed under the wrinkles of age.

"I hope I am tonight, my dear," she replied with a soft chuckle.

Other nurses entered the room, and finally my mother was able to come in too.

"We all know what is at stake; we may only have one shot at this," Dr. Mary said to everyone. She gripped my mother's hand for a fleeting moment, and then Mom was asked to step to the edge of the room. Dr. Mary ran her hand through my sweat-soaked hair before putting on her exam gloves.

"I know you have been such a brave boy tonight, but do you think you could be brave for just a little bit longer? Would you do this for your mommy and me?"

I might have been young, but I knew "brave" was code for more pain. I looked to her and lethargically nodded my head. I could try.

"I promise, when I am done we can all have ice cream before we go to bed tonight. How about that?"

Although exhausted, a smile formed on my face. Dr. Mary unwrapped a needle, and a nurse came close to help. Gently, Dr. Mary brought the sharp needle up to my neck, and paused.

"Levi, I need you to hold very, very still for me, okay?"

My lip quivered as I nodded my head.

With the skill of one gifted by God, she slid the needle through my skin. Immediately, the vein rolled and, even in my dazed state, I squirmed at the sharp pain of the needle as Dr. Mary shifted the tip under my skin. She bit her lip in extreme concentration as she probed for the elusive vein. Then she stopped.

"Got it!"

The room broke into a quiet cheer as Dr. Mary stood up. She hugged my mom, who immediately broke down in her arms. Dr. Mary came back to me and leaned down, offering one last kiss on my forehead. Exhausted by this final ordeal, I peered through half-closed eyes at her loving, smiling face.

"I am so very proud of you. You are such a brave boy."

The IV skirmish was over, the blood transfusions and other medicines began, and my life was spared.

Over the coming months, the new treatments were successful, and the cancer retreated in remission. I gradually returned to life with increasing vitality and joined activities with other young boys. Even though I was not in public school at the time—a precaution, since my immune system was still susceptible to disease—my mother allowed me to play on our neighborhood YMCA T-ball team. Turns out, I wasn't too bad at it.

To celebrate winning my fight with cancer, both Dr. Woods and his nurse Maxine came to a few of my games. The worst days were behind me; it was time for my family to return to normal life. Once again, things appeared hopeful.

4

MOM

L ife is so very fragile. One second we are here in our prime, the next we are gone, remaining only in the memories of friends and family. We live each day, never knowing what will happen next, as everything that lies beyond the horizon is mystery. Only One knows the future and what truly lies in store for us beyond our hopes for tomorrow.

⸺⁓⁓⸺

I was in remission. Yet, almost before we could get normalcy underway, two events occurred that left my family forever changed. And all we could do was close our eyes, hold tightly to each other, and pray that the nightmares would stop.

The first incident happened when I was eight years old. My grandmother Betsy died from a heart attack. She was in her early sixties and was the rock of our extended family. A woman of deep strength who had lived through the Great Depression, she had worked in a steel mill during the Second World War. This was the woman from whom my mother inherited her culinary skills. There was nothing in the world that my grandma could not cook to perfection.

She always seemed so much younger than her actual age, a soul radiating life and humor. She would often chase me, overwhelming me with hugs and kisses, and I adored her! Some of my fondest memories come from the times I slept over at my grandparents' house. Grandma Betsy would cook a large plate of fried chicken accompanied by an enormous bowl of mashed potatoes and gravy. Gooey chocolate brownies covered with vanilla fudge-ripple ice cream were the traditional dessert. At night when she tucked me into bed, she would tell me a story, followed by an outpouring of her love for me.

"You are the toughest and most handsome man I have ever met, Levi. There is not a thing in the world you cannot do if you put your heart into it!" This was my grandma—always bringing out the best in everyone. Back then I believed the world was held together by her love.

All this would end, though, I believe because she was a pack-a-day smoker and had been since she was a young girl. Her death had us reeling against the ropes like one of the boxers I'd seen in the Whatsoever gym.

But it was the second event a year later that delivered the knockout blow to our fragile life. My family and I and the way I saw the world changed forever. And like everything else, there was nothing I could do to stop it.

In the middle of a chilly November night, I woke up to screaming.

"Levi! Levi, wake up! Something's wrong with Mom!" the shriek of my sister's voice rang out from across the hall.

I sprang out of my bed and dashed into the room Misty and Mom shared. Wide-eyed and pale, my sister held on to Mom, who convulsed violently from one side of the bed to the other.

"Run! Get help!"

I stood frozen for a few seconds, watching the horrific scene, then I snapped back to reality and ran for the phone that hung on the kitchen wall. My little fingers dialed the only number I knew.

"9-1-1. What is your emergency?" Clipped and professional, a woman's voice came over the line.

"There's something … something's wrong with Mom." The words flew out of my mouth before I even had time to think.

"Do you know your address so we can send an ambulance?"

"I think … it's on Walnut Street. I'm not sure." I paused, desperately grasping at the address hidden away somewhere in my mind. "Please help!"

"We have a unit on its way, son, stay on the line."

I had to help Mom, so I stretched the cord as far as I could down the hall into my mom's room where I handed the phone to Misty.

"I'm getting Ginny!" I yelled as I ran out of the room.

A steel door in a short hallway separated our duplex from the adjoining one. Seconds later I pounded it with my clenched fist.

Our elderly neighbor opened the door, rubbing sleep from her eyes.

"Ginny, something's wrong with Mom! She's not waking up!"

With a tired yet urgent nod, she tightened her robe and followed me into our house and down the hall to the bedrooms.

"Levi! They can't find us," my sister said, setting the phone down when we came into the room. "The dispatcher says they can't find us!"

My brain wrestled with what to do. Then I got it! At least it had worked in Jurassic Park. I threw open the hall closet door and dug around until my fingertips found a flashlight. Wasting no time, I ran out the front door into our yard. The wail of the ambulance siren sounded like a few streets over. I turned on my makeshift searchlight and pointed it into the air, waving it from side to side. The bright beam illuminated the underside of the low cloud cover.

The sirens went silent for a second and then turned back on. I took that as a sign that they had seen my light and were heading our way. I kept waving the light until the ambulance pulled up in front of our house. One of the medics jumped out and trotted toward me.

"Son, your mother. Where is she?"

"In the bedroom," I said, pointing toward the open front door.

Inside the house was a scene I wish I'd never witnessed. Ginny and Misty had brought Mom out of the shower—her seizure had caused her to lose control of her bowels. Sitting wrapped in a bath towel was a woman who looked like Mom, but was wild-eyed and unfocused.

One of the paramedics knelt down, gave her hand a small squeeze, and said, "Miss, how we doing?"

My mother lethargically stared at him. The paramedic shot a glance at his partners.

"Ma'am, do you know where you are?" he tried again, shining a tiny flashlight into her pupils.

Mom just sat there, mute. The paramedic nodded his head to the others, and they began loading her onto the waiting gurney. The paramedics rolled my mom outside, as one of them pulled Ginny and my sister aside and gave them some instructions. I followed the men with the gurney.

"Don't worry, son," one of the men said to me right before he stepped inside the ambulance. "We'll take good care of your mom."

As the ambulance sped off down the street, I still didn't know what was going on. I stood on the porch, barefoot in my pajamas, and tearfully waved good-bye to Mom.

Misty called Aunt Tracy, and she made it to the emergency room as Mom's initial exam was finishing. The ER doctor tried to send Mom home with Tracy. He suspected it had only been a nightmare and that she was fine.

It only took a minute for Tracy to see this was not her sister sitting there semicatatonic. Not only did she have several cracked teeth from the seizure, but she'd gone to the bathroom on herself. My aunt refused to take my mom home until more tests were done by a different doctor.

The second report yielded dramatically different results. A CAT scan showed my mom had suffered a severe cerebral hemorrhage. An aneurysm had split and was bleeding in her brain. She was immediately admitted and sent to the ICU.

Mom wasn't coming home.

Tracy walked through our front door as dawn's light filtered through the living room window. My sister and I lay curled up together on the couch.

Tracy sat next to us and carefully explained what had happened and what this meant for our family. Surgery was scheduled for a week from now, and she needed us to pack a few overnight bags. Until Mom came home, we would be living with her.

Every day after school, Tracy picked us up and we all went to the hospital. A few days into this nightmare, Mom had a second aneurysm, worsening the tear in the ruptured artery. The doctors put her into a medical coma to keep her resting after that. Our afternoons together, we sat in the hospital room and watched my mom lie motionless in the bed. The echoing beeps and chirps of the hospital machines were the only signs of life.

Each time a rescheduled surgery was growing close, my mother would have another hemorrhage. After the third one, the doctors brought her out of the coma so we could spend some time with her awake. Yet this was not our same mom. The woman who sat there didn't resemble the strength and love I'd known. This wasn't the mom who'd held me when cancer racked my body, or who had draped her hair over me during that first terrifying spinal tap. Nor was this the mom who cooked spaghetti dinners pro athletes envied. I wanted *that* mom back.

When we walked in after school one day, Mom was sitting in her bed watching the television. Several times during our visit, she tried to speak, but her words were slurred and unrecognizable. However, one time she did speak clearly. It was a question addressed directly to me, her little boy, the man of her house.

"Am I … going to die?"

She had my hand grasped firmly in her own as she looked to me, then to my sister and Tracy for the answer. Before we could answer, she squeezed my hand, as if to say to me everything would be okay, no matter what happened.

Words stuck in my throat. Finally, I worked up enough muster to get words flowing again.

"No, Mom, everything is going to be all right. I promise!"

I wish my words could have prophetically written the pages of our life.

⚉⚉⚉

Aunt Tracy came to pick us up, but today was different. Her eyes were bloodshot, and she was silent as she helped me collect my coat and backpack from the classroom since school wasn't even over yet. Misty was already in the backseat, and no one said a word. We drove to the hospital as we did each day, but the closer we got, the heavier the weight on my chest. Something had changed, but I was too scared to ask what.

When we cleared the lobby doors, I knew the answer.

Grandpa Harold, tears streaming down his loving face, swiftly came to us.

"I'm so … s-orry!" he sobbed, as he plucked me off the ground and tightly held me in his arms.

It was over. Mom—our mom, *my* mom, was gone.

Silently, we walked down the labyrinth of halls toward Mom's room. Tracy held my sister's hand, and I clung to Grandpa Harold's. As we stepped into the room, my uncle Stan stood from a chair by my mother's bedside, and we all embraced and cried.

A devastating final hemorrhage had stolen the very essence of our mother, leaving her body alive but empty.

One by one, we took turns in the room, saying our good-byes. When it was my turn, I came along her bedside. Light from above the bed filtered down onto her angelic face. I reached for her hand and looked at the woman whose love and life I adored.

Eerie beeps from the life-support machines chirped around us. I clung to her warm, motionless hand, hoping this was just a bad dream. *It's time to wake up now*, my soul screamed. Only we weren't going to wake from this.

Gently, I climbed onto the bed beside my mom. Still holding her warm hand, I leaned forward and kissed her on the forehead, the way she had done countless times to me.

"I … *lo-ve* you!" I whispered, sobs choking my words. I couldn't seem to draw enough air, and I tried to keep from throwing up. I laid my head down on her chest and cried.

Sometime later, the rest of my family came back into the room. We all stood there as the finality of the situation weighed us down. A team of nurses entered and stood alongside us. One of them walked over to the machine that was keeping my mother's body alive. She looked to my grandpa and, by his hesitant nod, switched off the ventilator, ending my mother's life at forty-two years old.

⁓⁓

My mother was gone, and there was nothing any of us could do about it. *Nothing*. She'd lasted just three weeks after her first aneurysm.

This was the moment our lives came crashing down. And it was the day my family began to fall apart.

We left the hospital and returned to my aunt's house, where we spent the rest of the day crying and mourning our loss. I sat by myself, staring out the window in the guest bedroom, accompanied only by the suffocating pain of a lost loved one. The world could have stopped spinning and I wouldn't have noticed. Truth was, my world *had* stopped spinning.

On November 26, 1993, at the age of nine, I spent the day after Thanksgiving laying my mother to rest. Many people came to pay their respects, and the funeral home was standing room only. The key men of my family gathered to carry Mom's casket to the hearse, and, at Grandpa Harold's insistence, I took the place as head pallbearer.

The funeral procession drove along under a gray rainy sky that matched our mood—a caravan of bright headlights and heavy hearts heading to the cemetery beyond the city limits. Once there, I huddled in my seat in the front row of chairs under the canopy of the weather tent. Clouds of breath puffed silently as the pastor recited the eulogy.

I suppose the words were meant to comfort and encourage, to provide peace and hope. But my heart wasn't receptive to the message. In only a few months, both my grandmother and mother had been ripped from our lives, leaving holes that could never be filled. Those holes were deep inside me, empty craters where love had once lived and now only fear remained.

I stared up beyond the leaden sky all the way to heaven. "God, whoever you are … *wherever* you are … I don't ever want to talk to you again!" I muttered between clenched teeth and tight lips so no one would hear.

※

At the time of my mother's death, I didn't blame God. I didn't *like* him much, but I didn't blame him. However, as the days went on, I sure would. Being raised with Judeo-Christian values, I knew who God was, knew the power he had. He could have saved Mom, the same as he had saved me back when I had cancer. Yet for some reason, my mom's life was not spared, and I wasn't going to let him forget that he'd failed.

From the funeral on, I carried a chip on my shoulder, toward life and toward the One who could have moved heaven and earth to save my mom.

Now a grown man, I look back and laugh at my foolishness—the thought that I could hold God accountable for what happened—but at nine years old, this is exactly what I was planning to do.

Even as I was giving up on God, he was not even close to giving up on me. My life would be undeniably interrupted by His passion and love, and, as the days ahead unfolded, he would prove just who he was.

5

PEANUT BUTTER SANDWICHES

Is God really in control when everything crumbles around us? It's hard to believe it in our moments of desperation, but he is. We are human, finite, and not all knowing. We are not awesomely good either, proved by our ability to utterly mess things up every time we are given the chance. Then, illogically, we blame God. We put a massive fist in God's face, charging him with our condition, all while propping ourselves up with shoddy human theologies.

One day, even if it is not until we stand before him, we will see him for who he *really* is. I was just a child, and I still had a long way to go toward learning this lesson.

<hr/>

The day we lowered my mother into the ground, I went to war in my heart with the One who rules over heaven and earth. Convinced it was all God's fault, I stomped like a child throwing a temper tantrum right to his throne and laid the blame at his feet. Then I turned my back and walked away. He could not be trusted to keep his end of the deal to look out for me.

In the weeks and months to come, I retreated from life. Whether I liked it or not, every facet of life was changing yet again. Aunt Tracy bought a house in our school district, and Misty and I moved in with her. School became something I simply endured, staring blankly out the window while my teacher scratched meaningless symbols on the chalkboard.

Misty was a sophomore in high school and old enough to handle the changes far better than I. Blue-eyed with sandy-blonde hair, Misty often dressed like a tomboy, and for a while she was into the grunge look from the nineties rock culture. Still, she was plagued with social anxiety and preferred the seclusion of her bedroom, where she dug into her homework, the reward of straight As giving meaning to her life. Or maybe this was the way she numbed out. Eventually, she harnessed her fears and became heavily involved in theater and debate.

We grew up together as brother and sister, though we never really connected. As strange as it sounds, I actually never saw much of her, and while the Whatsoever center meant so much to me, Misty hadn't spent much time there. Although we were siblings by blood, we were very much strangers under one roof.

School was my constant amid all the turmoil and all the changes. Tracy found her own solace in her career. She'd put in long hours at the firm, and we hardly saw her. Often she would arrive just in time to pick me up from the after-school program before it closed, and then we'd race home to eat dinner, clean up, finish any homework, and then straggle off to bed—just to do it all over again the next day.

Tracy did the best she could in the beginning, having been thrust into the role of a midforties single mom of two growing kids. She did what she could to make the adjustment easier for us, from buying all the brand-name clothes we could fit into—radically different from the hand-me-down rags we were used to—to whatever gadget or toy either of us wanted.

What I *really* wanted was Mom. I was old enough to understand loss. And having witnessed death repeatedly, I knew what crossing that grim line meant: the person wasn't coming back. This time it was my mom who wasn't coming back, and my heart was left undone. I began to shut down.

⁓

Misty would barricade herself in her room, doing whatever it was she did in there, and my aunt sequestered herself in her office each night after dinner, working on brief or trial documents for her firm. So I was left to wander the house by myself—and think.

Not long after we moved in with Tracy, my grades tanked. Most days I simply sat and stared out the window or drew some make-believe land on the notebook in front of me—a place where I was happy, a place called home.

For many months after Mom's death, I hardly said a word. The only person who could get me to speak was my grandpa. Not only was my mom gone, so was almost every facet of her life: pictures of her, clothes she wore that lingered with her scent—everything that would remind us of her was boxed up and never found its way to our new place. It was like she had never existed.

It's how my family deals with pain: when something hurts, you ignore it; if there are mementos, you put them away; forget about it, and it will eventually go away. Out of sight, out of mind.

But this wasn't true for me. I didn't want to forget about it, forget about *her*. Our family's coping was too much for me to handle at ten years old.

I wasn't the only one. I watched as Aunt Tracy, one of my best friends and one of my strongest encouragers, changed before my eyes. She was no longer fun, and we never played or laughed together anymore; she just locked herself in her office and did her work. I was too young to understand she was dealing with grief in her own way, so I took it personally.

———

Once again, I was the man of the house by default. College was still a long way off for me, so I didn't need to worry about grades or the other things Misty had to focus on. In turn, I was given the bulk of the chores after school. Beyond the dishes, cleaning, and other work, I longed to feel wanted again, to feel a part of something and important to someone.

I longed to be loved. Yet my heart felt only empty pain. Less than a year into our new lifestyle, I reached my breaking point. One day after school, Misty picked me up because Tracy was staying late at work to brief for a trial the next day. As usual, my sister went to her room, shut her door, and cranked up her rock music.

Left to myself, I knocked around the house for a while. But that's all it had become: a house. It held people I knew and loved, yet it wasn't a home. It wasn't *my* home. I wanted a family, and I knew where to look.

I snuck into the garage, pulled my bike off the wall, and hit the door opener. Its mechanism rattled loudly but was drowned out by Misty's blasting music. I wheeled through the neighborhood to my buddy Adam's house, not far away.

After hiding my bike in the bushes, I ran up the steps and rang the doorbell. A few seconds later, Adam's mom, Deanne, answered the door with a surprised look on her face.

"Levi, hon, what are you doing here this late?"

"Can I live with you guys? I really want to have a family again."

She looked like she was about to cry, and I grasped that as hopeful.

"Tell you what, kiddo, why don't you come inside and I'll make you a snack."

For a little while, we sat at the kitchen table with a plate of peanut-butter sandwiches, and I sat on her lap. She lovingly wrapped her arms around me and talked to me about all the feelings that had been ignored the past year, and she cried along with me. Though she could never replace my mom, it felt good to be held, to be rocked, to be loved. Finally, I had found a home again.

Ding-dong! Deanne went to answer the door. Tracy stood on the porch, a ticked-off look on her face.

"Thank you for taking him in, Deanne," she said, as she stepped into the house and turned her attention to me.

"Go wait in the car until I come out," she snapped.

Uh-oh. I'm in for it now.

Tracy stayed behind and talked with Deanne for quite a while before she came back out to the chilly car. She had barely shut the car door before the scolding began.

"Why would you do this?" she exploded. "Do you realize what an embarrassment this is? I had to leave in the middle of a brief because of this stunt. What were you thinking, Levi? Can you please tell me?"

"I ... I do-n't know. I just ... I just want to go home." Tears flowed freely down my cheeks. Yes, I wanted to go home. But that place didn't exist anymore.

She slammed the gearshift into drive, and we drove in silence. For some reason we passed our house and pulled out onto the freeway.

"Where are we going?" I asked, still racked with sobs.

"To the hospital, Levi. You've left me no choice. You need help."

My stomach sank. *The hospital. Like the cancer place?* I thought of all the pain I'd experienced there. And the hospital was where Mom died.

We rode in silence for the duration of our drive, and I looked out the window onto the moonlit scenery of the Kansas City landscape. A little while later, we arrived at a large building, but this wasn't Children's Mercy or Mom's hospital.

I followed my aunt into the building's lobby, trying to figure out where we were. Tracy pointed me to a chair off to the side. She continued to the front desk.

The staff member got up and came over to me. "Levi, would you please follow me?" she asked politely.

Together, the woman and I walked down the hall and stepped onto an elevator that took us a few floors up. Once the doors opened, we walked some more, beyond a door where a nurse sat behind a glass window. She buzzed us into the locked area, where the nurse asked me to sit in a side room. She left for a minute, then returned with a pitcher of water for both of us.

Confused, I sat while she made a few notes in a file with my name across the top. Finally, I worked up the courage to speak. "What's going on?" Lumps had formed in my throat, and my voice sounded like a fog.

"Well ... that's what we need to figure out, Levi," the young nurse replied, flashing a fake smile from across the table.

"I don't have cancer again, do I?" I asked, hoping to everything I didn't.

Puzzled by the question, the nurse's brows furled. "You had cancer?" she asked, as she stopped making notes.

"I did, but I don't anymore. Wait. Where's my aunt?"

"She's gone home for the night. She'll come by in the next day or two to see you."

"She *left?* Wait ... where am I?"

"Regions Hospital, and you're going to stay here with us for a bit so we can give you the help you need."

She kept talking, but my thoughts drowned out her words. *Why did my aunt leave me here, especially without saying good-bye?*

I found out later that "here" was a psychiatric hospital where I'd undergo an evaluation. Whether I liked it or not.

⌐∿∿⌐

The hospital, by design, was supposed to be helpful, but it felt more like living in an animal cage surrounded by nightmarish people. Most of my fellow patients were much older and were dealing with their own issues. It wasn't the type of place for a young boy to make friends. One young girl ran around screaming that the mailbox would steal your soul, and we were all going to die, since the world was coming to an end. Most nights one of the patients could be heard screaming. I admit, the place scared me.

Thirty days came and went before the hellish nightmare ended. That's when my aunt came to pick me up. We sat together in the same room I had first come to on this floor. A doctor and one of the nurses joined us.

"Clearly, your nephew is hurting," the doctor said to my aunt. "He doesn't know how to process everything that is going on presently in his life, let alone what he has already been through."

Tracy sat in her chair and dispassionately listened to what he was saying.

"Levi needs a healing environment; one where he is with those he knows and trusts—a place that is loving; one that will let him grieve. In ten years of life, he was ignored by his father, was molested, survived cancer, and lost his mom. The human psyche just isn't built to handle these kinds of successive traumas, especially not at such a young age."

Our meeting drew to a close, and the doctor encouraged my aunt to take me home to a more supportive environment. If she could work fewer hours and spend more time with me and my sister, together as a family, that would be best.

Comfort was what the doctor ordered. When we returned home, things deteriorated further. Many nights I sat in my room alone, waiting for Misty to come home. When dinner was over, I had chores to do. Then it was time for bed.

To make matters worse, some nights I could hear Tracy and Misty in the living room, laughing while they watched television together after my bedtime. Most nights I cried myself to sleep.

I realized that if I wanted love, I had to take it.

One night while I was doing the dishes, Tracy walked into the kitchen. As I heard the sound of her footsteps draw close behind me, I jerked my hands out of the soapy water, turned around, and threw my arms around her to catch her before she could get away.

Crash! A bottle shattered on the tile floor. Red wine—an expensive cabernet—sloshed from my aunt's glass and was soaking into her silk blouse.

Tracy peeled me off and pushed me aside. "Look what you did!" she yelled.

"But ... I love y-ou." My lips trembled.

She rushed to the sink, grabbed a dishcloth, and fervently wiped her shirt.

In a frustrated voice, I heard her whispered words: "I just can't love *you right now.*"

Devastated beyond words, I ran to the bathroom and crawled into the bathtub, flinging the shower curtain closed around me.

My nightmare was confirmed. I was unwanted, unloved—*alone.* I was so tired of being alone. I curled up on the floor of the tub and sobbed loudly. "I want ... my mom ... I wan-t to go *home!*"

That's just it. There was no home. No mom.

The bathroom door creaked, and suddenly the shower curtain flew aside.

"Go! Get your backpack, put some clothes in it, and get in the car ... now!" Tracy jerked me up onto my feet and pushed me into the hall.

I had already lived this scene before, only this time it was a different facility, and I sat by myself in the after-hours waiting area of this one-story building. When someone finally came to greet me, it was way past my bedtime, and I sleepily followed the faculty member back to the treatment room. We went over the same song and dance as before.

Several hours passed before I was taken back to my room. After changing into the provided scrubs, I climbed into the strange bed and clung to my pillow, burying my face in its sterile-scented, scratchy cover so no one could hear me weep.

It was the moment I knew I was going to be alone in this world, whether I wanted to be or not.

Unwanted. Uncared for. Unloved.

6

SHATTERED
HEARTS

Rejection. Loneliness. Abandonment.

These words defined my life, as inch by inch I slid toward the abysmal black hole consuming my heart. I was caught in a dangerous minefield—nowhere to turn, no place safe.

I let go of the hope that I'd ever feel loved again. After all, who was left to love me? I was just a child, and life had become a grudge match: me against the world.

~~~~~

About another thirty days passed, and my aunt came to retrieve me. The diagnosis was the same. *Heartbroken.*

Once again, Tracy was encouraged to become a hero to my heart. The woman I had been so close to since birth, who had held me the moment I first drew breath, was now only someone I used to know. There couldn't have been more distance, or pain, between us.

When we left the psychiatric facility, I thought we were heading home, but when we pulled up to Regions Hospital, I knew this wasn't over. Like a messed-up rerun, I walked alongside my silent aunt into the lobby. I guess this was the only place left for me to go.

I sat in a corner staring out the window as snowflakes drifted across the parking lot, my soul too numb to shed a tear. Tracy talked with the same staff as before.

This time Tracy joined us as we traversed the hallways of this godforsaken place. We rode the elevator up a couple of floors, to the same security door as before. A team of nurses and a doctor greeted us inside the conference room just beyond the checkpoint. Tracy paused briefly before she spoke.

"I'm sorry, but I can't do this ... I can't raise him," she said, dabbing her eyes. "I wasn't prepared for this, to raise kids. With his sister, it's different—she goes to college in two years. I can do that, but not this. I'm sorry. "

That was it. Tracy wiped her face and left the room, stepping onto the elevator the second the doors opened. No good-bye, no *I love you*.

***

Now, just like my mother, Tracy was gone. But instead of death ripping her away from me, this time it was her choice to leave, and that tore a raw, bleeding hole in my heart.

I stayed at Regions for a few weeks until a new home could be found. Behind the scenes, Tracy relinquished legal guardianship of me, and I was handed over to the system and the courts. I had a new status now: *ward of the court.*

All this really means is that an attorney, one whom you will seldom if ever meet, becomes your de facto parent. You become a case file, one more name scrawled on a manila folder locked away in some file cabinet. You almost cease to be human. You become a legal—if not actual—orphan.

There was one man, though, who stepped into this void—someone Mom hadn't spoken kindly about, but who was blood relation to me nonetheless. And I was about to go live with him.

***

Uncle Stan, who'd been in the room when my mother died, came to pick me up from Regions Hospital. His house would become my new home.

Although family, I'd only seen him a few times in my life: family get-togethers, cookouts, the day I began chemotherapy, and only once since Mom's funeral.

Stan was a quiet man in his late forties, with a flippant, comical attitude that reminded me of the actor Alec Baldwin. Stan was narcissistic to the core. He'd been a teacher at a local inner-city school and was superintendent for the Kansas City, Missouri, school district—a district where there were more fistfights and dropouts than passing grades.

Like most of the remaining people with whom I shared DNA, Uncle Stan kept to himself. When he wasn't working or writing a book for the school district, he was in the basement studio recording music, *his* music, a passion he carried from his days as a hippie teen during the 1960s.

Toward me, he was cold, distant, and uninvolved. I felt I could have disappeared off the face of the planet and he wouldn't have even noticed.

His family life was complicated and full. Around the time of Mom's death, he remarried for the fourth time. He had two sons with his first wife, my cousins Kolt and Erik, and two daughters with his second, whose names I didn't know. Only Kolt lived with him.

His new wife, my step-aunt, Brenda, had three kids from her second marriage: Chloe, Tyler, and Grayson, and they lived with Stan and Brenda.

Life at my uncle's house was a huge adjustment. There were no rules, no boundaries, and no expectations.

"If you skip school too much, you'll end up in juvenile hall, and I guarantee you won't like it," Stan said that first day. "You know when dinner is on the table. Other than that, do whatever you want. Doesn't matter to me—you're not my kid."

Yeah, that was my uncle's house: every man for himself. A lot like growing up in the Wild West.

The next few years I spent in his house, but it was on again, off again. Two weekends a month, all five of us cousins would clear out to give Stan and Brenda some alone time. The other kids went to their other respective parents' houses; I was left to go to some other relative's house. Most times I was able to go to my grandpa's.

I'd barely gotten my footing at Stan's when Stephen, my dad, came back around. This time he was trying to get full custodial rights. He was still the same old man with a tricked-out muscle car, Marlboro cigarette dangling from his lips, and the last beer still fresh on his breath. It was years later, and he still couldn't call me by name. As always, I was "Little Buddy."

I might as *well* have been living on Gilligan's Island. My life was a fantasy, a houseful of people I sometimes doubted even knew I existed. And now I was suddenly required to hang out with my dad whenever he felt the urge. As usual, my uncle didn't care, as long as I was out of his way.

I was reeling against the ropes again, waiting for my tap-out.

Amidst all of it, though, one person would step in and be a force of hope, of love. Grandpa Harold was coming to my rescue.

7

HOMESICK

Love.

One word. Yet undeniably powerful!

Within milliseconds of reading it, your brain has already fired off a barrage of emotions and thoughts. And your response is based on your own experience with love, good or bad.

Love is such a commanding aspect of our lives that the quest to find or hide from it has driven mankind to the ends of the earth.

From the womb—whether we are aware of it or not—we long for a love that will forever accept, forever embrace, and forever remain. It is what we are created for.

When my mom passed, I fell into a loveless existence. That's until Grandpa Harold stepped in. He became the closest thing to a father I have ever known.

After Grandma Betsy died, Harold married Eleanor, a longtime friend from church. Eleanor loved me as much as Betsy did, and I delighted in visiting them. Their house became a place for my heart to call home.

On my weekends away from my uncle's, I'd stay with them. Harold always found ways to show me love, from taco night at the local VFW, to after-hours card games at the Moose lounge with friends of his, veterans of either World War II or Korea. Together, he and his old war buddies treated me as if I was just another one of the guys. Every time one of them ordered another beer, they'd shout to the barkeep, "Get Harold's boy a soda, too!"

Harold's boy. I liked that. Finally, someone wanted to claim me.

Those nights, as we played a game of *Thirty-one* long past my bed-time, we shared many laughs together.

After the day had turned into the next, and the guys had one too many drinks, the stories began—bedtime stories not fit for boys *or* men. With red eyes and slurring speech, they recounted the places, firefights, and friends lost in their service for our country. Each one of these men had scars, and the ones they wore on the outside of their bodies they proudly showed off. Badges of honor—mementos for having put it all on the line for each other.

Despite the decades between us, we all became friends. They were just a bunch of boys trapped in bodies bent by a lifetime of memories and age.

Staying with my grandparents forged memories I will always cherish deep in my heart. On Saturday mornings, I woke to the smell of my grandpa's pancakes wafting throughout the house as he walked around humming some tune from his youth.

In the hot summer months, we played croquet on the back lawn. On a rainy day, it might be a game of darts in the basement. Whenever we could, he and I sat on the back steps with our shirts off, soaking in the sun while we devoured a plate mounded with sliced watermelon.

Evenings were spent on the front-porch swing as my grandpa and I rocked back and forth, gazing down the street at the sunset in silence.

Those days I will always hold dear in my heart. Harold, my grandpa, was the most loving and God-fearing man I've ever known. Those weekends with my grandparents were never enough. I wanted to live there all the time! My visits with them were warm and loving. But I knew my real *home* was at my uncle's.

My stomach sank the moment my uncle pulled into my grandparents' driveway on Sunday evenings. I wished Stan would forget where I was and leave me there, but that never happened.

Each winter, my grandparents took off for a couple of months to some vacation spot on the other side of the world. I had school, so I could not go with them. That left Stan to find someone else to watch me on the alternating weekends. The choice was always a distant relative, generally one of my aunts or uncles from my Grandma Betsy's first marriage (before Harold). Usually, I'd stay with Aunt Roxie and my cousin Wyatt.

∼∼∽

Two of my cousins, Kolt and Wyatt, were members of a gang. Though the two of them had seldom met, they were carbon copies of each other. Gangbanging was all they lived for. Except for the weekends with my grandparents, I was exposed to their influence and that lifestyle on a full-time basis.

When I was at my uncle's, I was eager to please and get Kolt's attention. Even though he was only a teenager, he was the alpha male of the house. He was too wild to tame, so my uncle let him do as he pleased.

Then on the weekends I had with Aunt Roxie and Wyatt, he became the de facto big brother I had always wanted.

A young boy, fatherless, surviving the loss of a mother, and crying out for affection and love … well, you can probably see this one coming a mile away.

∼∼∽

Roxie and Wyatt lived in the *rough* part of Kansas City, blocks from where I was born and raised. No matter which direction you looked from their front stoop, you saw nothing but a cold, cruel ghetto of depravity and poverty.

With a crack house on every block, the law of the land was, *"Mind your own. Watch your back. Don't run your mouth."* Do that, and you might just live to see tomorrow. It was a gangster's paradise and was also hell on earth.

Oddly enough, that neighborhood was my cousin Wyatt's domain. A true thug at heart, Wyatt didn't have the wherewithal for anything but hustlin', and at sixteen he was a high school dropout. The only responsibility he took seriously was keeping up with his probation officer.

At about six feet tall, Wyatt stood head and shoulders above me. He was a grown man with a boy's mind.

He looked the part of a thug, too. Muscled up, loaded with tattoos, and a faded-up flattop, he had a scar that ran alongside his head from a car accident. Even though he appeared tough, he was all brawn and no brain, like a human Rottweiler. The one exception was when it came to avoiding the cops. Then he became the street's MacGyver.

When I stayed at Aunt Roxie's, I became Wyatt's shadow. And he wasn't ashamed to have me tag along. To him, I was his "cuz," and with that came the respect of his friends.

He, too, was family, and he looked out after me as such. That attention and affection was all that was needed to pull me in. At eleven years old, I eagerly followed Wyatt into a gang member's life.

Wyatt and I had this routine when I was there. Roxie would leave for her night job shortly after dinner and, when the coast was clear, he and I would hop onto a pair of tricked-out, chrome mongoose bikes and roll out to join the rest of his entourage at a park a few blocks away.

No matter the weather, we were out on those streets, and we believed we owned the neighborhood. Each night we'd run up and down all the blocks surrounding his house, busting each other's chops with the latest "yo mama" jokes—except none were ever directed at me for obvious reasons—using language that would get most kids a bar of soap in the mouth.

One of us always carried the portable boom box on which we blasted the latest Tupac or Biggie Smalls track. Along our way, we routinely stopped off at one house or another so Wyatt could offload drugs for a fistful of cash. I always ended up carrying the backpack with the crack in it. The crew's reasoning was: "If the po-pos bust you with it, Levi, they can't take you to jail. You's too young." I believed this. It was my way to be a part of the crew, so I went with it.

When we weren't selling drugs, we picked fights. We were always picking fights.

Wyatt and I never made it back to his house for the night. When it got late, Wyatt would post up at some house for the night, often the last house we sold drugs to. We would drink and smoke into the early morning hours, while others took hits off a crack pipe downstairs or had a girl off in some room. Wyatt was often too messed up to even care where he dropped his head, so we would bunk there at the last crack house.

A *crack house*! Not really a place I wanted to be, let alone go to sleep. So I didn't. Those nights, I kept my eyes half-open, pretending to sleep, but really I was watching out for myself and my cousin, who was passed out.

The houses were filthy, smelly, and dangerous, but the people there accepted me. I was Wyatt's cousin, so they took me in and treated me like I belonged. This felt good; it was what I craved.

My new aspirations came from watching Wyatt and his crew. From wearing the hand-me-down basketball jerseys he had outgrown to the brand-new, hundred dollar Michael Jordan sneakers, I did what I could to emulate him. I even let Wyatt's girlfriend shave the sides of my shoulder-length hair and braid the top into cornrows.

Gangsta rap music became a staple of my life and was all I would listen to. I even went so far as to carry a butterfly knife in my pocket everywhere, sometimes even to school. I had become one of them.

Was this all it took? The slightest hint of no-strings-attached "love" and I was headlong into a thug-boy's life. My heart was fooled into believing that I'd found fulfilling love on the streets with my cousin.

Once again, life was about to give me a dose of whiplash. My dad, Stephen, was pushing harder than ever for full custody. The courts were warming to the idea, and they gave him a chance to prove himself.

Not long into my sixth-grade year, he was given permission to pick me up whenever he wanted, for however long he wanted. When he'd come by, we always did what he wanted. Usually, that was going to the park to toss a football around. Being a high-functioning drunk, he had the motor skills to pull it off, even when you could taste the beer that floated in the air downwind of him.

He tried his best to teach me what he knew about the game of football, even while he pulled another cold one out of the trunk of his 'Stang. He was born and raised in Texas, and football was god to him, so much so that his love of the game ran deeper than his love for anyone or anything else—except maybe alcohol.

My dad thought he could mold me into a stud player, and he taught me all the running plays and pass patterns he knew. I hated the pass plays because I rarely caught the ball. It wasn't that I was totally inept, but he threw with all the strength he had, so hard it would have turned a grown man's hands black and blue. Sometimes his throws knocked me down. When I dropped his pass—which was most of the time—his anger would build until he blew up, spewing a barrage of obscenity. He always ended it with, "*I can't believe you're my son!*"

I might not have been great at football, but there was one thing I was about to catch, and that was a welcome break from all this.

⸺⁓⁓⸺

The break was more like a longtime dream. Spring break came that year, and I went down to Brenda's brother and sister-in-law's home.

Their names were Jonny and Carolyn, and they lived several hours south of Kansas City, in a small town nestled in the Ozark Mountains. I stayed with them for the whole time, and they included me in everything they did. It was amazing!

And when it was time to head back to Uncle Stan's, Jonny and Carolyn shared with me that they were unable to have kids of their own and wanted me to be part of their family. They wanted to adopt me.

I was going to have a family again!

The remaining days of school were torture; each week dragged by like its own month. And when school was finally over, I was more than ready to launch into my new life.

I packed up everything at Stan and Brenda's and made the trip back to the Ozarks. It was time to settle into a home, once and for all.

Jonny and Carolyn were in their early thirties and lived in the middle of no-man's land in the Ozarks of southern Missouri. Their triple-wide modular home was set on five hundred acres of densely wooded ranch land—a boy's dream.

Jonny was a tall man, with a fair complexion and a crown of jet-black hair, and working on the property had given him a severe farmer's tan. He'd served in the Gulf War in the Marines and brought his training as a mechanic into the civilian world, where he ran an auto repair shop in town.

Jonny was a busy man, but when he made time for me, it was as if the world had stopped and I was the only one that existed.

Carolyn was tiny in stature, and she too had ebony hair. Thin lines of freckles splashed her skin. We had plenty of time together. She was a schoolteacher and was at home for the summer, grooming her skills as a stay-at-home mom. I thought they were the perfect couple, uniquely complementing each other.

The summer was filled with endless adventures. Jonny was often out on the ranch doing fence repairs, managing their large garden, or taking care of whatever else needed to be done. He welcomed my company and helping hand. Jonny taught me everything a young boy envisions when thinking of the wild: how to navigate the densely forested land, putting up a barbed wire fence, and what every boy covets—how to shoot a rifle!

I loved the smell of the crushed grass as we drove the fields, the cool shade in the thick stands of trees, and the taste of Carolyn's dinner when Jonny and I arrived home, starving after a long, hot day.

Many times he would even toss me the keys to the old rusty pickup and, with a childish smile of his own say, "Go on. Take her for a spin!" I'd crank the engine and take off on my driving adventure. Of course I had to sit on the two phone books he duct taped together to let me see over the wheel.

Jonny became the father I had always wanted!

⸺⧫⸺

Summer drew to a close, and my grandparents came to pick me up for the remaining few weeks before I started the new school year. I had been having so much fun in my new home that I had almost forgotten about them, but when I saw Grandpa Harold again, I realized just how much I had missed him.

The day before they were supposed to take me back home to Jonny and Carolyn, Stan called and told Harold to bring me to his place. My heart sank to my stomach as we headed to Stan and Brenda's house, something I so dreaded.

"Why are we coming back here?" I asked my grandpa as we pulled into the driveway.

"I'm not sure." His voice seemed uneasy, unnerved, and his expression tipped his hand. Something was wrong.

When we walked in the door, Stan called for us to join him in the living room. With a stern, unemotional expression, Stan shared the news that shattered my dreams. Carolyn was pregnant. With the baby on the way, I was no longer needed. I would not be returning there, to the place I thought would be home.

To add to my deep disappointment, I would be living at my uncle's again. I was right back where I'd started. Most of the time over the next several days, I locked myself in my basement room and sobbed uncontrollably.

One day I lay on my futon, my face buried in my pillow as I cried. *Thuddd.* The bedroom door came flying open.

"Will you shut up already!" Brenda barked. "Why are you such a child? Just suck it up and be a man. You're almost a teenager!"

I looked at her blankly, as if this was all some bad dream I would wake from shortly.

"Maybe when you realize no one wants you, you can find your peace, you little brat."

Those were lies. I knew where I was wanted.

"Fine! Let me go live with Grandpa Harold!" My voice shook as I spoke.

"You can't. He's too old, and he doesn't want you either. No one wants you!"

Boom. The slammed door emphasized her point.

Moments later she returned, still in her rant, and laid down my uncle's revolver on my desk. "Just do this world and yourself a favor and end this pathetic mess!"

She didn't say another word. She didn't have to. I knew exactly what she meant.

I sat there in my room and stared at the pistol. She was right.

I could end this mess—me—in an instant. It could all disappear.

Slowly, I got up and walked to the gun. I picked it up, surprised at the heft of the weapon, and watched the light reflect off the shiny metal. Sickened by her gesture, I went upstairs and put the handgun back where it belonged—in my uncle's nightstand.

In the following days, Brenda was very verbal about her desire that I not come back to live with them. Then again, she had been opposed to me coming from the onset, back when Stan first picked me up from Regions Hospital. Most of the times I saw her in the house she ignored me, even when I spoke to her. Once she popped off, "I don't want you here."

She made a brazen threat: either Stan sent me packing, or she would leave.

Despite Brenda's tantrums, I moved back into my basement room. It was like retreating to a dungeon—dark, no windows, and a musty smell I could taste on the back of my tongue. The space was a mirror image of my heart.

Being unwanted ate away at my sanity. If I wasn't wanted at Jonny and Carolyn's, or here at my uncle's, where was I wanted? Was Brenda right about my grandpa too?

Did anyone want me? Did anyone love me?

⟿⟾

Amid the pain and unanswered questions, I came to find that someone did, in fact, love me.

Not long after I moved back to Stan's, I awoke suddenly in the middle of the night.

Something stood at the foot of my bed, something that looked like a Man engulfed in a mist of brilliantly pure light, a light that was falling ever so softly onto my bed. As it fell, I noticed I was wrapped in warm stillness.

Whoever this was, he was powerfully affecting my senses.

Whoaaa! What in the world—?

I sat up and rolled onto my knees, stretching out my arm so I could touch this Man. As soon as my fingers swirled through the mist, a powerful surge of warmth coursed through my body, like a hot fire pulsating through my blood.

Watery-eyed, I gently bit my lip. I felt something powerful and something desperately longed for. I felt ... loved!

I must be dreaming. I checked the iridescent red numbers of the

67

clock on my dresser—1:38 a.m. Still not convinced, my doubt was erased as I wiggled my toes in my socks.

"My child, you are not dreaming!"

Words so brilliantly clear, but not aloud, as if I had heard them in the depths of my soul.

Then I saw something in the light. *Love*. Limitless love. As if he wanted to show me something indescribable by human words.

It wasn't just sight; I *felt* it with every fiber of my being.

Teardrops slid down my cheeks, markers of a long-felt pain, now dissolving beneath the weight of this Man's love. Then came words I will never forget.

"Levi, I love you with a love beyond your understanding. I have always loved you, and I will never stop loving you!" His words whispered through my soul like a gentle breeze.

"Wherever you go, I will always be with you, by your side, no matter what!"

Undone by who I saw standing before me, I leaned forward to latch my arms around him in a long, ached-for hug.

Before I could fully reach him, his light brightened, blinding what my eyes saw, as if reaching deep into my heart to show that he too was embracing me.

Gently his words carried into the chasms of my soul. "There are many things you will walk through in the days ahead that will be very hard on you, and they will break my heart. Know that I will be with you always, no matter what, to the end, and I will never stop loving you."

Our moment was so brief, so fleeting, but one in which I knew I was touching eternity, an eternity where love will never cease.

I looked into his face.

"Now it is time for you to fall back asleep, my child."

A longing for this moment to continue gripped me, as something beyond my homesickness spoke that he—this *Man*—was my home.

A place of refuge, of safety. A land that I longed for and an existence of endless love. A home where I would always be wanted and where I would always belong.

"No, please … don't leave!" I choked on my words. "Please take me with you!"

I felt a great pressure on my eyelids, and I felt myself slipping back underneath the covers, as if he was tucking me back into bed.

"My child, now is not your time to come with me," his words soothed. "When it is time, I will come for you. I promise!"

I clung to this moment as long as I could, watching as the Man slipped beyond the void of my closed eyelids.

Once again I was sound asleep.

Loved! Someone loved me! In the years to come, I would see just who this love was.

8

ALL ON MY OWN

Who was that man? Was that … *God*? Countless times since that experience, this question has lingered inside me.

Could he, or should I say *would* he, really come to me like that? In the middle of the night, to my bedroom, just to speak to me? If so, what would he say?

That he loves me?

⁓⁓⁓

The next morning after my encounter with this love, I slipped upstairs for breakfast. My uncle sat in the den next to an open window, a crisp newspaper pinched between his fingers. It was his daily routine during the summer months.

"What's the face for, Levi?" Something about my countenance must have been different, enough even for him to notice.

I approached him, clueless whether I should share this with him. Then again, he was blood.

"Well." I cleared the nervousness from my throat. "Something happened last night. I mean, someone came to me, in my room."

"Someone came to you? Who?" he asked, sitting up straighter.

"Yes. I mean I think so. He looked like a man, but was made of this foggy light, kind of like the sun was his body." Even as my words fell off my tongue, goose bumps rippled along my neck.

"There was a person made of light in your bedroom?" he said, stifling a snicker.

"I, um … think so?" My heart sank at my uncle's mocking undertone.

"Why didn't you call out for help or something? Weren't you scared?"

"I dunno? It was … too awesome," I explained. "It said it … loved me!"

Stan's laugh finally broke out as he tossed aside the paper. "Levi, you mean to tell me that a person made of light stood in your room, only to tell you it loved you?"

"Uh … yeah. I mean … I guess so," I said hesitantly.

Excited, my uncle leaned forward. He wanted me to tell him more. Unable at the time to see through my uncle's façade, I eagerly shared with him the events of the night before. Besides, why wouldn't I share it with him? He was my uncle, after all. And this was the most interest he'd ever shown in me. Uncle Stan listened intently as I told him all I had seen and heard.

Later that day, he had me ride with him on a few errands. Parking at what I thought was another place on his to-do list, he led me into an office building and opened the door to a doctor's office. Actually it was a psychiatrist's office. My uncle had made an appointment for me.

After I was asked to retell everything that had happened the night before, the doctor scolded me. "You didn't see or experience anything but a vivid dream or hallucination. This is common with people in grief; your subconscious just wanted to see your mom again." He looked at me over his glasses. "Young man, I assure you it is scientifically impossible for you to see or experience what you described. The best thing is to forget it. If you fantasize about it, you'll make it into something it's not. I'll give you some medicine to help."

I guess that was that! At least to the doctor and my uncle it was. Our next stop was the nearest drugstore to fill a prescription for a hallucination medicine. Stan parked the car in the lot and turned to me.

"Levi, you are one messed-up kid," he said, ripping into me. "What are you trying to do? Do you just want some attention or something?"

Torn to pieces by what I perceived as betrayal, I stared out the car window, doing my best to ignore him.

"Look at me. Are you even listening to me? Do you want to be a lunatic? Because that's what you're becoming," he snapped, opening the door to get out. "Maybe it would've been better for you to die from the cancer." With that he stepped out and slammed the car door behind him.

I watched in the side mirror as my uncle walked away, waiting until he was in the drugstore before I broke down. I barely got the car door opened as my stomach heaved. Half-digested food splattered on the asphalt. Grabbing a napkin out of the glove box, I wiped off my mouth and eyes so he wouldn't know he'd caused me to cry.

My uncle returned to the car and tossed the bag of pills in my lap. He told me how and when to take them. And that is what I did.

For the rest of that summer I lived in the windowless basement, waiting for junior high to start. I never again mentioned my experience with the being of light, and I suppose my uncle thought the pills cured me. But I hadn't forgotten that night in my room when a radiant cloud of light crept across my bed and enveloped me in a cloud of love. I buried the still vivid memory deep down in what was left of my heart.

<hr />

During the second week of school, I stepped off the after-school bus to see that my uncle was home early from work and sitting in his candy-red sports coupe. Rock music blared from the open windows as he sang along. When the bus had roared away, he turned off the noise and called for me to hop in. He was off to a friend's house for dinner, and I was to join him.

The car ride seemed like an eternity as we drove far beyond the outlying suburbs of Kansas City and into rural Missouri. Our destination, a small log cabin on top of a hill, was nearly quarantined by the long, winding gravel driveway that my uncle's car climbed. As we reached the top and got out, an older man and woman came to greet us. The man stuck out his hand to my uncle.

"Howdy, I'm Earl Petersburg." They shook hands. "And this is my wife, Anne."

My uncle had lied to me. Friends don't shake hands and introduce themselves. This was my uncle—always a card up his sleeve and never to be taken at face value.

Earl and his wife urged us to come inside their old, dilapidated cabin and have some dinner. We took our seats, and I sat quietly as dinner was served and listened as the adults talked. I kept one eye on my uncle. Clearly he was up to something.

With the meal behind us and conversation thinning, my uncle thanked them and motioned for me to follow suit. We climbed back into his car and left. The drive home, already long, was made longer as Stan cranked up his tunes so loud my eardrums pulsed.

"Stan, who were those people?" I asked over the deafening noise. The question came from my gut, and it was telling me something wasn't right.

No reply. He kept his attention on the tune of the song. I didn't matter to him. Very little mattered to him. I turned back to the world sliding by outside my window.

∞

The next day, I gazed out the school bus window as we rolled down my uncle's cul-de-sac. My fingers gripped the seat as I sat up. A strange car sat on the driveway. A woman stood beside it, watching my uncle loading stuff. Wait … that was *my* stuff!

My heart lept in my throat. I stumbled down the steps and onto the road. The bus pulled away behind me as I walked slowly to the scene. No one acknowledged my approach.

"What's going on?"

The woman, who had poked her head into the trunk while she arranged items, turned to me. Her mouth opened slightly, as if to offer an answer, only to turn to my uncle with a look that said, *You take this.*

Stan shifted the box of my stuff in his hands and, with an annoyed tone, snipped, "This is Glenda from Social Services."

"O-kay?" My palms began to sweat. I knew what Social Services was, and my brain began putting two and two together.

Glenda stepped toward me and put her arm around me in a hug. "I'm sorry, Levi."

Annoyed by this woman's touch, I brushed off her arm and stepped away. "Sorry for what?" I asked, but I directed my question to Stan.

"Glenda is taking you to a foster home."

"She's *what*?" Words erupted from my mouth with little thought.

"Don't you get it?" Stan roared, now steaming with anger as he threw the box into the trunk. "We don't want you here!"

Without offering another word, he turned his back and went inside—presumably for another box of my belongings. I turned to Glenda and stretched my arms wide in frantic disbelief.

"Come on, honey, let's go. We don't need to make this any worse than it already is." Her words were foolishly hollow. She didn't even grasp what she had just said. Then she reached for me again.

"Get off!" I barked, the fury rising inside me. "I'm not going anywhere with you! I don't even know you!"

It was the wrong time to speak my mind. Stan had come back outside with the last of my stuff, and he was done with all the drama.

"Shut up, Levi!" He strode to the car, shoving the box into the cramped sedan. "It's time for you to be a man and go your own way!"

Stan grabbed my wrist as if to motivate me into the car faster. Furious, I ripped loose and backed away, never taking my eyes off my uncle.

"No! I want to call Harold! Let me call Harold, now!" Red-hot teardrops of anger dropped onto my shirt. I stepped toward Stan. "Does he know about this, that you are doing this to me?"

Glenda stepped between the two of us, palms raised. But my words had fallen on deaf ears. No, not deaf … just uncaring.

"Forget about it." My uncle turned his back and stalked off.

Glenda gave me a sympathetic look. I was trapped. I couldn't call my grandpa for rescue, and I had to go with her to foster care against my will. Over her shoulder, the man who had been my uncle walked into the house and slammed the door behind him. Like Aunt Tracy getting on the elevator, Stan never looked back.

Destroyed, I collapsed in a heap on the edge of the driveway.

Glenda stood there with her hand on my shoulder as I sobbed.

This was the last time I knew the word *family*.

※

Our drive was a hard one, and I had no clue where I was going. For most of the trip I sat staring numbly out the passenger window, trying to focus on a world passing by beyond the pane of glass and not on my own pain. But my stomach twisted in violent, rolling knots.

Glenda did the best she could, given the situation, and tried to comfort me with small talk and the occasional "Everything will be okay," and "You'll like your new home."

Despite her compassion, her words were utterly foolish, and anger rose within me. Like my new home? How would she know? She'd never been in my shoes. Besides, that's just it, nowhere was home—not since Mom. That's how this whole mess began.

As if the day hadn't already been painful enough, we pulled into a familiar driveway that twisted and climbed up a hill. At the end of the gravel road was the Petersburg house.

Betrayal swirled inside the chaos of my heart.

He had lied. My uncle had lied to me. Why?

⸺⸱⸺

What was left of my family was now gone. My own blood had given up on me and left me to find my own way in this world. Alone.

Like air from a slowly leaking balloon, the last bit of hope for a life and family leaked away that day. No one could do this life alone. And that is exactly what I was.

Alone.

9

THE SYSTEM

God, are you there? Where are you when the world is falling down around me? Can't you see what is going on?

Don't you care? Why are you letting this happen?

I was twelve years old, and life was yet again eroding around me. Where was God?

~~~~

One month into the seventh grade, I found myself in foster care. I was unneeded, thrown away by my own *blood*. They had disowned me.

The Petersburg house was secluded, with only one neighbor for miles around. The only chance I had to relate to other kids my own age, let alone anyone else, was at school. And this was my new home, whether I liked it or not.

I didn't like it.

The house was an old, shoddy log cabin, with three small bedrooms, kitchen, bathroom, and a living room. But that didn't make it a home. Earl had just hit seventy and had a long, snow-white beard. White hair with rust highlights sprouted from his head. Aided by his deep chuckle and saddled with a stout potbelly, he would be the hands-down winner of any Santa Claus look-alike contest. He was half-crippled from a stroke a year earlier and now spent most of his days in the recliner by the window, watching some televangelist on the television.

Anne, the same age as Earl, was more physically active and came across as a sincere woman. But she'd been born with a debilitating speech impediment, and it took me quite a while to understand what she said. I had to learn her body language and mannerisms to get the gist of what she meant.

Their ten-year-old granddaughter, Darcy, lived there too, and with the four of us it was very cozy. Not too long after I moved in, it became ridiculously overcrowded. Ryan, Max, and Christopher—all foster kids and new to the system like me—joined us. Ryan and Max were twins, and Christopher was their younger brother. Their family had been busted for a meth lab in the basement, so Social Services took them away.

A girl, Melissa, came at the same time as the boys but was of no relation. Now sixteen, she'd been a foster child most her life. Her mom had been a prostitute and crack addict, and other than a few visits at the penitentiary, Melissa barely knew her.

The boys bunked in my room, which was barely big enough to jam a pair of beds in it, with a narrow gap between them for an aisle. Two beds and four boys: that's easy math—we shared.

Darling granddaughter Darcy, though, had the run of the house. Her mom had died in a car accident when Darcy was young, and her grandparents were her only family. She was short, freckled, and plump. A mat of thick, greasy hair sat above a pair of thick glasses, and if she used perfume, it had the dank odor of unwashed feet. Worse than her hygiene was her snotty attitude, barking orders at anyone who came near. And even with the house's space constraints, she refused to share "her" room—the biggest bedroom in the house—leaving Melissa on the living room couch with a suitcase as her closet. Unjust? Yeah, but I would come to learn that this was the "system."

Melissa, a high school sophomore, was the kind of girl that, when she walked down the hall, boys stopped to stare and girls huddled in groups to whisper. Blessed with radiating good looks, a friendly temperament, and a vivacious personality, she came across more like a grown woman than a teenage girl. And Melissa always kept up to date with the latest fashions. But despite her warmhearted nature, she often expressed that her life was doomed from the start and how she longed for it to be over.

In a way, I knew how she felt, and the two of us instantly bonded.

With Anne and Earl running around to corral the endless energy of the boys and meet the ceaseless demands of their granddaughter, that left Melissa and me to fend for ourselves. So we'd vanish, always unnoticed and without complaint from Anne and Earl.

Our one neighbor, Chloe, was the same age as Melissa. She was beautiful, with shoulder-length black hair always pulled back into some sort of creative mess held together with a pair of black chopsticks. Chloe was artistic and had a different pair of fake glasses for every occasion and mood. She said it made her look more astute. I wasn't sure what that meant, but it sounded brainy.

Chloe had her driver's license, and her offer of a ride in place of the school bus seemed like a godsend, even if she seldom went to school. Her folks ran an adult gift shop in Kansas City, and they worked late nights, leaving Chloe to do as she pleased. And what pleased her was rummaging through the liquor cabinet to her heart's content and pillaging half-smoked cigarettes from the ashtrays scattered around the house.

The week of Thanksgiving break, I stepped off the bus and began huffing up the long gravel drive that led to the Petersburg home. The diesel engine of the bus grumbled off into the distance, leaving a pungent cloud of choking exhaust that dogged me as I hiked. At the top of the driveway sat a car I'd seen once before. Glenda, my social worker, got out and made her way to me while pulling her coat collar up against wind-whipped snowflakes.

I stopped short when I saw her backseat was filled with my belongings. "I'm moving again, aren't I?" I asked Glenda, strolling past her and toward the house, as if her being there with my possessions meant nothing.

"I am sorry, Levi, but yes, you are." Her face was remorseful and her tone sweet.

I kept my stroll for a few steps before I half turned to face her. "Yeah? What if I don't want to?" I deepened my voice to mimic my rebellious stance. "What have I done now?" I had barely resumed my march to the house when she called out to me, her voice weighed with concern.

"Honey, wait! It isn't you!" Although several feet away, she reached out as if she could hold me back from entering the house. But my gut told me to go inside, so I did.

Anne was sitting in the kitchen, eyes red and a pile of wadded tissues in front of her. Earl stood from his recliner when he saw me. He strolled stiffly toward me, draped his large hairy arm over my shoulder, and told me what had happened.

Melissa had stayed home from school with a stomachache.

They found her hours later, unconscious in the bathtub, wrists slit and her lifeblood running into the lukewarm bathwater. An empty bottle of aspirin lay nearby, and a suicide note was centered on the bath mat.

She was in the hospital in critical condition, but the doctor was guardedly optimistic.

I slipped away from Earl's grasp and sank onto the living room sofa. Why would Melissa do such a thing?

But I understood. Pain. A heart *full* of pain. And through my experience walking the life I had in just twelve years, I understood: Melissa had tried to escape the pain the only way she knew how.

Because of her actions and the overcrowding at the house, Glenda felt it was best I be placed in a different home. With a hug from Anne and a few waves, I said good-bye to the Petersburgs, climbed into Glenda's car, and went to my new home.

For the fifth time that year, I was changing the place I called home, not that any of the places I lived meant that anymore. I was forced to adjust; I simply had to since I had no say.

The drive was quiet. I didn't want to talk, at least not to Glenda. Even though none of this was her fault, I didn't like her much.

My second foster home was in Grandview, Missouri, a southeastern suburb of the Kansas City metro. Within hours of getting off the school bus at the Petersburgs', I was introduced to total strangers.

The Chadwicks—Jeff, Tammy, and their two-year-old, Emma— were to be my new family. They lived in the not-so-nice part of the city in a recently built home that already had a worn feel, as if the neighboring buildings were sucking the life out of anything new.

Jeff was a delivery driver for Frito-Lay, while Tammy was a stay-at-home mom who ran a day-care center out of the house. Jeff was generally gone by dawn, often working extra shifts and returning long after sundown. Tammy watched over the seven kids left with her for the day.

Despite an outwardly nice appearance, my gut told me this wasn't going to be a good place to live. And my gut was seldom wrong.

Tammy was morbidly obese, and her days consisted mostly of sitting on the couch and bingeing on soap operas while the kids ran around doing whatever they pleased—which was usually thrashing the house. Shortly before parents arrived at five o'clock, Tammy would get up from her post and scramble through the house to get everyone and everything presentable. As soon as I moved in, Tammy made it my after-school responsibility to get everything cleaned up and ready the kids for their parents.

But an hour after school was never enough time for me to get all the other things done that she wanted. So around four o'clock each morning, Tammy would come to my room to make sure I got up and finished my chores before school. The work went beyond simple chores. There were unwashed dishes left over from the day before, and they were piled nauseatingly high on each of the counters and kitchen table. I was greeted each morning with the smell of spoiling food.

By the time I was done, I usually had enough time to take a shower and sprint to the bus stop. Sometimes I didn't make it and watched the red taillights of the bus pulling away in the distance. On those days, Tammy never offered to take me to school.

"Tough luck, kid! Looks like you're stuck here today with me."

This was the punishment for not making the bus, her company and chores, which always consisted of me taking care of the kids for the entire day while Tammy watched her shows.

~~~

Moving in with the Chadwicks and playing the role of housekeeper wasn't the only kicker. I was one of only five Caucasian students at my new school, and I was the only boy in that group.

I'd grown up in an African-American neighborhood where whites were the minority, but this was different. It was almost like my presence there was a threat to the other boys my age, so they would pick fights with me. It started on my first day.

A tall boy wearing drooping shorts sauntered up to me as I gathered my books from my locker. Before I knew what he was up to ... *whoosh!* My pants fell around my ankles. The boy laughed, and those passing by in the hall stopped and joined him. Blood rushed to my face, and I leaned over to pick up my pants.

Thwwackk! His fist struck the side of my head. As he backed off, a barrage of curse words aimed at me rolled off his tongue. I didn't know the kid, nor had I seen him before, but he clearly didn't like me.

Forget this. I stood up, flashed a mocking smile, then drove my knee into his stomach and watched as he doubled over from the pain, his own face turning red in the process.

I'd just balled my fist to hit him in his mouth, when a hand grabbed me from behind. He had friends—several of them. In seconds I was under a pile of kicking, stomping feet.

It wasn't too long before a teacher came to drag us apart, but not before I'd made enemies. Each week I found myself in some fight or another, almost always outnumbered by eighth-grade boys. It didn't take long for me to grow used to this, nor did it take long for me and my big mouth to antagonize them even more.

The school principal called Jeff and Tammy plenty of times, but the calls were never returned. Many days I came home with a black eye or swollen lip, but neither Tammy nor Jeff asked about it. Eventually came the day the principal thought enough was enough and suspended all of us for one week.

That got our attention, but it didn't really bother me. I had figured out what worked: close my eyes and numb out. My punishment for being suspended was no different from my regular day-to-day routine at the Chadwicks': clean this, wash that, and "go chase after" the day-care kids. I learned to play the role of an adult, everything from keeping the kids calm and entertained to changing overflowing diapers. And I had to learn it on the fly.

When the suspension ended and I went back to school, things mellowed out. Seems a couple of the boys' dads had set them straight.

One of them even apologized profusely, as he sported a swollen cheek of his own. Seems his home life wasn't so great either.

Most days I'd arrive home from school and Tammy would leave me with all the kids and take off for the Taco Bell down the street to get something to eat.

A typical Midwest winter arrived right on time that year, the air a harsh slap of subfreezing temperatures every time I ventured outside. I had been living at the Chadwicks' for a month when a new boy, Carlos, moved in with us. He was seventeen and fresh out of juvenile hall. The courts were using the Chadwicks' as a halfway house of sorts. Since Carlos had a job at Bannister Mall, not far from the house, he was there only at night.

Like I mentioned before, the Chadwicks' house suffered from lack of basic upkeep, and you didn't have to look far to find something broken or worn out. In my bedroom, the north-facing window had a chunk of glass missing from when it had been broken long before I moved in. Strips of duct tape had been stuck over the gaping hole, but the bone-chilling wind had curled the tape's edges, and cold shot into the room like a frozen knife with the slightest breeze.

My room was small, and Carlos and I crammed into it. My bed happened to be right by the window, and the silver tape wasn't doing the job. The pane needed to be replaced. Cold and desperate for warmth, the two of us took our appeal to Jeff and Tammy in hopes of a new window. Only it fell on deaf ears.

"Quit your whining!" Tammy said. "Be big boys and suck it up. Unless you want to be the ones to buy a new window."

Forced to take matters into our own hands, Carlos and I raided the stockpile of blankets downstairs and made a mountain of blankets to sleep under each night. For additional insurance, we stayed fully dressed and sometimes slept in our winter coats. It sure beat freezing to death.

On the weekends, Carlos sometimes invited me along with him to his job. We'd catch the Metro bus down the block and ride it to Bannister Mall. I found out the first time that his "employment" was hustling drugs. When we were done with "work," we would head to the food court or arcade.

I was young and naive, and I looked up to Carlos. He reminded me a lot of my cousin Wyatt, and with all the distractions to keep us entertained at the mall, we became close friends.

Only our friendship didn't last long. Six weeks after we met, Carlos was hauled away by the police. He had been busted shoplifting at the mall. When the cops searched him for more stolen goods, they found marijuana and crack cocaine in his pockets. He was going back to jail, and this time he'd be locked away until he was a grown man.

With Carlos gone, it was once again up to me to watch my back—even in the Chadwick house.

Foster care dragged on, a monotonous life of indentured service. Like countless mornings before, I got up well before dawn to clean up the waiting kitchen mess: a whole day's worth of dishes and trash cans overflowing with foul, soiled diapers. The room resembled a landfill, and I had the role of a ghetto male Cinderella.

Some days Tammy called the school and told them I was sick so she could run off with some friends on a shopping spree. On those days, I had to hold down the fort—and the day care—all by myself. I crawled into bed each night with the nauseating realization I would have the *privilege* of waking to the same thing the next day.

I *loathed* life.

It didn't take long, sleeping next to the drafty broken window, for me to get sick. I developed a wracking cough, sore throat, and a fever. A trip to the doctor's office revealed I'd come down with bronchitis. We came home from the jaunt to the doctor's office and drugstore to a stinky house and a flashing light on the answering machine.

Child Protective Services had left a message: they were stopping by first thing the next day. One of the parents of a day-care child had reported the Chadwicks. Her poor kid had developed a severe rash from sitting around in a soiled diaper all day.

Tammy flew off in a tirade of anger and curse words. It was my fault, all of it—the phone call, the child's raw backside. I was her convenient scapegoat, but I didn't care. I was sick and just wanted to take my medicine and go to bed.

In the middle of the night, the overhead light switched on and flooded the room. Tammy stood in the doorway.

"Get out of bed, you little brat!"

She crossed the room, grabbed my arm, and dragged me out of my warm cocoon. I followed her to the front door. She yanked it open and pointed beyond the frosty storm door.

"Van's unlocked. You can either sleep in there or out on the street. Your choice—I don't care." Blood reddened her cushy cheeks. "See you at four!" She tossed a winter coat at my feet seconds before the front door slammed shut, accented by a distinct clicking sound of the locking deadbolt.

Stupidly, I sat on the front porch, thinking she was bluffing, tightly wrapping my arms around me as I alternately shivered from the arctic night and sweated from the fever.

But she never came back to the front door, even when I annoyingly knocked on it for some time.

She hadn't been bluffing. I could either sleep in their minivan out on the street, or …

I had an idea. It was late, but I could see a glow of lights down at the end of the road. Tammy's favorite haunt, Taco Bell, was still open—at least the drive-thru—so I took off in a jog. My bare feet were frozen stumps by the time I arrived and stepped up to the drive-thru window. I rapped my clenched fist against the glass, and a young woman slid it open.

"Can I help you?" She was clearly puzzled why an adolescent boy would be standing in the cold barefoot. I could see a clock on the wall behind her. It was after 1:00 a.m.

I had only gotten out a few words of what had happened with Tammy when she motioned toward the front door and told me to come in. I slid into a booth on the much warmer side of the windows, and the young worker handed me a cup for the soda fountain. She flashed a friendly smile, then said she'd be right back—she had a quick call to make.

When I returned to the booth with a fizzing cup of Sprite, I found a wrapper of fresh cinnamon twists.

I had died and gone to heaven!

I was only halfway through my sugary treat when a police car pulled up outside and parked. It wasn't rocket science to figure out why they were here. Once my host let the two officers inside, one of the men came and sat across from me, while the other stopped and talked to the girl.

"Son, what are you doing out this late?" The cop's tone had a hint of sincerity.

I pulled away from my snack. "My, uh, foster mom kicked me out."

His face didn't change. "Yeah, that's what we heard." He glanced at his partner and nodded toward the cruiser outside. "How 'bout this? You hop in the warm car with us, and we'll make sure you get back home safe?"

"No thanks. I'd rather sit here and eat cinnamon twists."

The cop's voice dropped an octave. "Kid, you don't have a choice in this."

Of *course* I didn't. I never had a choice in anything.

"Now come along with me, and let's get you home for the night," the cop said, rising to his feet and waiting for me to do the same.

Still half-asleep, Jeff wasn't pleased to be awakened in the middle of the night and greeted at the door by a pair of police officers with me in tow. Jeff was clueless—he often got home from work about the time I crawled into bed—and he stood there with a tired, annoyed expression on his face as he listened to the officer talk.

Then Tammy came to the door; she must have learned how to act from all the soaps she watched. Tammy explained I had been sent to bed early that night, grounded because of my grades and for always getting into fights at school. I was a troubled foster child and must have run away once everyone had fallen asleep.

A troubled foster child?

Her performance was Oscar-worthy, and she fooled everyone—except me. After a brief lecture by the cop, the two of them left me in the care of the Chadwicks. Jeff sent me to my room, and I slid under the mountain of blankets. They were stone cold, but my thoughts were warmed by the kind girl and the cinnamon twists.

I had just drifted off to sleep when Tammy came into my room angrier than before. She told me to follow her to the kitchen. Sitting in the middle of the floor was a bucket, bottle of dish soap, a couple of old crusty rags, and a toothbrush.

"Get to work!" she barked, before disappearing into their bedroom.

I slumped. It was 2:30, and I wasn't going to get any sleep.

—⁓⁓—

I made it through class the next day half-comatose, and I knew I would return to the same mess at home I always did. But I was in for a surprise.

When I came home, there was a man sitting in the living room, having a pleasant conversation with my repulsive foster mom. The two of them laughed at some joke he told.

"Levi, go pack a bag … you're going to stay with some friends this weekend," Tammy said sweetly between her snorting chuckles.

I didn't have to be told twice. Not just because I hated this house but because I'd figured I was going to come home to pick up where we'd left off early that morning. In record time, I stashed clothes in my school bag and returned to the living room. The tall stranger stuck out his hand.

"Hi, Levi. I'm Allen Bochner." A chiseled grin accented his soft-spoken words.

I rode in his car to the other side of Kansas City, where he and his wife lived. He was taking me for the weekend for something called respite foster care. I found out later it was to give the foster parents a break. But right then, I thought the break was for me.

The drive gave us a chance to get acquainted, and he didn't seem half bad. I actually liked the guy. Allen and his wife, Lorain, were unable to have children of their own; adoption was the only option to fulfill their hopes to start a family. The couple had met the Chadwicks months ago in a foster-parenting class.

Allen had asked Jeff and Tammy if he and Lorain could take me home for a weekend to see what it was like, to get a feel for this whole thing. I was just happy to get out of the Chadwicks' house.

I learned that Allen and Lorain owned a gift shop on the opposite side of town, so they were always on the go. And they must have had some money, because Allen pulled the car into the driveway of a beautiful home in a ritzy neighborhood. The roomy, four-bedroom house had an in-ground swimming pool in the back of a pristinely landscaped yard. It was nice digs, something I had never experienced before.

As a couple, they were a breath of fresh air to all who I had come to know in the past few years. Allen was middle-aged, tall, and solid muscle. He was also highly educated and often spoke in sentences peppered with large words requiring a dictionary for me to decipher. Despite his intelligence and intimidating appearance, he was very gentle.

His wife, Lorain, was about to hit forty, and her hair had turned completely gray a decade or more too soon. We stood almost eye-to-eye—at this point, I'd grown to about five feet six inches. She was also quiet, and sometimes I wondered how she and Allen conversed at all.

The Bochners were different from my uncle and from Jonny and Carolyn. Allen and Lorain took time to *be* with me, to know *me*.

Like I *mattered* to them!

We ordered pizza, actually sat together to eat, and watched movies. They even took me out to show me around the historic parts of town I never knew existed. I really enjoyed myself, to the point that I nearly forgot the reality that lay beyond the other side of this getaway.

Like all truly good vacations, the weekend didn't last long enough. My stomach roiled as we drove back to the Chadwicks'. When we pulled into the drive, Lorain turned to me from the front passenger seat.

"Here is our number, Levi. Call us … anytime. I mean it!" She smiled and handed me a piece of paper with the scribbled number.

I smiled in thanks, glad to have a connection with normal people again. Friends. However, down deep I feared this would be like all the others—they too probably wouldn't last.

⟞⟝

Coming back to the Chadwicks' that night was like stepping into a parallel universe. It was more of the same: foul odors and nasty attitudes. Tammy had a chip on her shoulder bigger than ever. Social

Services had shut down her day care until further notice. One too many times someone had called to report her for neglect, and now her income was gone.

"This is all your fault!" Tammy screamed, pointing her finger at me.

I hadn't even been back an hour. We were all gathered in the kitchen for Chinese food, which was likely a couple of days old. Tammy paced around the room, screaming four-letter words and slamming cabinet doors.

Jeff shooed me out of the room with his eyes. Even though I was hungry, I went to my room and shut the door. I could hear the screaming across the house, and for the rest of the night I stayed in my room, out of sight and hopefully out of mind.

It seemed like only minutes later when I was jerked awake. Tammy stood above me, shaking my shoulder and swearing. "Get up and follow me!"

I followed.

It was 4:00 a.m. and the same old routine. The kitchen—always a disaster—was even worse after her earlier tirade. It looked like a tornado's debris field. A weekend's worth of pots and pans and dishes filled the sinks and teetered in filthy stacks; a glass had shattered on the floor, leaving shards glinting in the harsh fluorescent light; and napkins, spills of sticky liquid, and food scraps littered the floor. A mound of garbage surrounded the trash can, which probably hadn't been emptied since I'd left with the Bochners.

"This better be spotless by the time you go to school!" Tammy hissed.

I closed my eyes and swallowed as tears formed.

Maybe I'll catch a break when I'm dead. The day couldn't come soon enough.

Eleven hours later, I stood at the end of the driveway where the school bus dropped me off and simply stared at a familiar car and the woman beside it.

I took a few steps forward. "What are you doing here?" I clenched my jaw, trying my best to be nice. Poor woman never knew what to say, and I knew she was only doing her *job.*

"I'm sorry, Levi," Glenda replied, as her eyes misted.

I brushed past her and shot a glance in her car. Sure enough, my stuff filled the backseat and presumably the trunk as well.

"What's wrong with you?" I twisted away in frustration. "Do you enjoy this or something?" Even while I lashed out at her, I was torn. Part of me was thankful she'd come to rescue me from this pit, with its piles of garbage, smelly diapers, and drafty window. And Tammy.

But Glenda's presence reminded me she had personally delivered me to this very driveway, left me to face total strangers, and then driven away. Now it would happen again.

Regardless, I had to go with her. Just like that cop had said at Taco Bell: "Kid, you don't have a choice in this."

I didn't go inside the house. There was no point in saying goodbye. I didn't want to. I hated this place … maybe even hated Jeff and Tammy. My gut whispered something to me, something learned from experience. *The next place will be worse than the last.* I tried not to listen to it, but it had yet to be wrong.

As we settled into the car and I buckled up, Glenda looked at me and laid her hand on my knee.

"I really am sorry." A tear slid down her cheek.

I turned my head from her and exhaled, a forcible scoff, as if to say, "whatever."

I kept my gaze on the world beyond the window as we drove, my back half-turned toward Glenda, a sign of my disapproval. But my mind wasn't on her, wasn't on the unknown place we were going— someplace trying to pass itself off as *home.*

No, my thoughts were on life, and on God.

God, whoever you are, will you just end this, end me? Please. Life was hell, each cycle progressively worse than the previous, and I didn't want to live in it anymore. Still, a tiny bit of hope fought its way up through the muck of my crummy situation. Who knew, maybe this time I would catch a break.

Only time would tell.

10

THIRD TIME'S
THE CHARM

Instability.

This seemed to be the hallmark of my life at this point. Freshly thirteen years old and I was a nomad, a boy with no permanent place and no *one* to really call his own. Essentially, I was an orphan.

For the sixth time in a year I was moving, changing to my fourth school in the same school year, and starting over in my third foster home.

Third time's the charm, right?

One could only hope.

"I think you are going to like your new family, Levi." Glenda's words broke my resentful silence that filled the car like a fog.

"Yeah? What makes you think that?" Still numb and angry, I kept my gaze out the side window. The first two families hadn't exactly been Disneyland.

"Because I'm taking you to the Bochners' house!"

My head came up, wondering if I had heard her right. "Wait … you're what?" I turned toward her. "You're taking me to Allen and Lorain's?"

She smiled, meeting my eyes. "We're headed there right now."

For once she had finally gotten through to me, and I smiled in return. Was this really happening? Was I catching a break?

As we drove, Glenda explained that the weekend had been a trial run, not just in getting their feet wet to foster parenting, but also specifically with *me*. Allen and Lorain wanted me to come live with them.

The three of us would be a family. No more moving, no more drifting. I was finally finding a home.

The Bochner's welcomed me into their home with the same hospitality they had offered only days before, and they did everything humanly possible to make the transition a smooth one. I had my own room, one with a window that didn't leak, and the few chores they asked me to do were easy. The best news of all was they wanted to become my legal parents—rights and all.

A few weeks later, we traveled to the county courthouse to take the case of my guardianship before a judge. I stayed in a waiting room, while Allen and Lorain met with my court-appointed guardian ad litem. An eternity passed for me as a few other kids rotated in and out of the room, and a television in the corner ran an endless string of infomercials about "amazing" cooking grills and "unbelievable" spot cleaners. An ancient, dark-skinned man in a security uniform kept a watchful eye on us.

As the time wore on, fear crept up in my gut, and I grew more and more restless. *Had they changed their minds? Were they waiting for Glenda to come pick me up?* I wasn't going to let that happen. I walked over to the officer.

"Excuse me, sir. Do you know where my foster mom and dad are?"

The old, weathered guard poked his head up from a half-completed crossword puzzle and hummed in contemplation.

"Give me a second, young man, and I'll find out."

A few moments later he returned and plopped back down into the swiveling desk chair. "Son, they will be out shortly; they're waiting for your father to sign a few documents."

What?

My heart stopped and started again in the same beat, and sweat began beading on my forehead. "Sorry … Sir, did you say my *father* was here?"

The gruff old man chuckled. "*Is* here, young man. Jus' around that corner."

I stood frozen as thoughts swirled in my head. "Can … I please see Stephen … I mean my dad? Can I see him?"

The security guard tilted his head to one side, the deep creases in his face appearing to deepen before my eyes as a long minute passed. A tic, or perhaps a weak smile, signaled that he understood—like he'd been there before himself. He nodded. "Sure, youngin', I can do that for you." Once again he disappeared, and for a long time I kept my gaze on the doorway for any sign of my dad.

What was I thinking? Why ask to see a man who'd never really been there for me in the first place? Maybe there was something deep down that needed settling once and for all, that needed the closure of a good-bye. I waited, at once both anxious and hopeful, wondering if there could be anything between us. After all, we *were* father and son.

An hour later, Lorain came to the room. The guard still hadn't returned. I stood up, hesitant to move to her. "Where's my dad?" I asked, but I anticipated the answer.

A puzzled expression crept over her face. "He left some time ago and went home."

I hung my head. I couldn't believe it. Then Allen joined us, and we all walked together to the elevator.

"He probably just got lost in this place," I mumbled. Lorain draped her arm around me.

No matter how hard I tried to rationalize my dad's actions, the truth was self-evident. My dad left without ever saying a word—no *good-bye* and no *sorry*. Just like the day I was conceived. Why was he like this? Sometimes those answers never come.

I never saw or heard from him again.

⁓

The pain I felt that day was nothing compared to what was to come.

On an unseasonably warm spring day, Allen and I stood on the back deck under a cloudless sky, sodas in hand. Fragrant smoke rolled off the charcoal grill.

"Go get us a plate for the burgers," Allen asked, as he flipped the well-done patties over.

I drained the rest of my root beer, then slipped quickly into the house. As I returned with the plate, my stomach gurgled from the sloshing drink.

Grrurrpppp. The belch forced its way out of my throat as I held out the dish.

Wham! Allen slammed me into the railing, sending the plate in a high arc. It shattered into a dozen pieces on the deck's surface.

"Do you have to be so crude?" His eyes were lit with unreasonable anger. "Are you a foolish child?"

Nervously, I chuckled as I replied, "Uh … no … I'm sorry, Allen." I was still speaking when another burp came—right into his face.

Allen's fist drove into my mouth, and small sparks flew through my field of vision. The coppery taste of blood covered my tongue.

"If you are going to be stupid and rude, this is what you'll get," he said between gritted teeth. "Now, go to your room, and don't come out until I tell you!"

He released me from his grasp and turned back to the grill as if nothing had happened. Stunned, I was frozen in disbelief and stared at his back. When I touched my swelling lip, my fingers came away sticky with blood. I crept away as quietly as possible, heading to my room as told.

I was glad I didn't encounter Lorain on the way, and I closed my door and dove onto the bed, burying my face hard in the pillow as I began to cry. I didn't want anyone to hear, especially *him.* I shook from terror as hot tears soaked through the cotton pillowcase. *This can't be happening, not again. Please God, not this—not now, not ever again. Can you even hear me?*

Even then, during my shaking and tears, I let a small sliver of hope take hold. Maybe something had gone wrong in Allen's day, upsetting him, pushing him close to the edge, and my behavior had been the final straw. His action certainly didn't match the man whom I thought had rescued me from a horrible foster home.

༄

Two bookcases flanked the fireplace in the den. Countless Bibles and theological books lined the shelves, but beige dust covered the tops, all but obliterating the gold edging of the holy books. Dog-eared pages were a testament to a life that had once been full of study and ministry.

I discovered he'd been a youth pastor for many years—that is until his career came to a screeching halt. He never mentioned why, and he was no longer that man.

After that first blow that night by the barbeque, the gloves came off. There was something—from somewhere in his past—that rose like a malevolent demon.

Perhaps I was a reminder of wrongs done to him in his past or wrongs he'd done to others, because my very presence in that house set him off. From a constant barrage of derogatory swear words aimed my way to random blows, whatever was lurking in his heart found an outlet on me.

Allen would often quote what he'd heard in his own childhood: "Children are to be seen, not heard." Eventually that became an unspoken rule in that house.

I didn't speak to him unless I was spoken to. I didn't want to, anyway—I was afraid. He became the most rigid of control freaks.

Seldom did Lorain ever say a word or move to intervene. She was probably just as afraid of him as I was. Though to her credit, once in a while when Allen was freakishly out of control she would scream at him, "Stop it!" But the thing is, when a rabid dog attacks, you can't talk to it—you have to put it down.

The only respite from the attacks was school. Yes, school was my safe place. Funny, I think I was the only kid in my class that looked forward to going to school each day.

Living daily with a ticking time bomb at home, I couldn't handle the homework load and keep on top of my grades. I was never an honor roll student anyway. Then my report card came in the mail: all grades were below average. This really set Allen off. He knew I could do better if I tried, so he figured he had to motivate me.

His idea of motivation was to come to my school later that week and shadow me the whole day, sitting behind me during each class. I was in the eighth grade, and as a foster kid I already felt like a freak. In each classroom, I was aware of the uneasy glances of my classmates—it was uncomfortable for all of us to have a quiet, eight-hundred-pound gorilla in the room. I was so scared that day I could barely function, and I did my best not to draw any more attention to myself. But my gut said this one day wasn't the end of it—he had something more up his sleeve. When school ended for the day, Allen drove away without offering me a ride home. I climbed on the bus as usual, but the ride home felt like a death march.

I hadn't even made it into the living room when Allen came striding down the hall. He put his foot down on top of mine and shoved me over, driving his knee into my abdomen.

"Why didn't you answer any questions in your classes today, Levi?" Saliva from his mouth showered down on my face as he swore at me. "Are you *stupid?*"

I didn't have a chance to answer as his right hook drove into my temple. I tried to shake it off and squirm out from under him, but he followed up with a left and two more rights.

At least, that's all I remember. By that time, I was lights out.

When I came to, I was still lying on the floor. Allen was gone. I sat up, head spinning and throbbing. As silently as I could, I slipped back to my bedroom, crawled behind the clothes in my closet, and hid. My whole body trembled so much I couldn't even cry. Curled up, I held myself perfectly still. Blood dripped from my nose onto my tennis shoes, and I wiped at it with my thumb, but it smeared into an ugly line. My life had become hell on earth.

Where was Glenda when I *really* needed her?

⸺⸺

In some twisted logic, Allen became overprotective to make up for the abuse. Not that one can really be *protective* while being maliciously abusive at the same time. He knew the exact minute the school bus dropped me off at home, and I had until 3:15 each day to call him at work and check in. It was his way of keeping track of me even when he wasn't around. And if I was late with the call, he would call the bus depot the next day to confirm any reason I might have.

I learned quickly not to lie or do things with other kids after school—to do so meant pain. *Physical* pain.

The check-in calls always resulted in a long list of chores he'd rattle off, enough to keep me occupied inside and out of view. He didn't want his secrets getting out to the neighbors.

Like at the Chadwicks', chores once again took a huge chunk of my day. And if I didn't complete everything on his list to perfection, he would conclude, "You were out playing with your friends, weren't you?" That was always followed by more hitting and punching. Pain.

I was damned if I did and damned if I didn't. This really was hell.

About a year after I moved in, Allen and Lorain adopted two baby girls: Ella, seven months old, and Zoey, only one month. Why the two of them adopted girls, I don't know.

I was required to help take care of them. Actually, I pretty much became their only caregiver, to the point where Ella's first word was my name.

Every day I had to get up and wake the girls, clothe them, and get them out to Lorain's car so she could drop them off at day care on her way to the shop. The afternoons consisted of Allen's work list as soon as I got off the bus, right up until Allen pulled into the driveway with the girls and I would take over from there. I was also to have dinner on the table by six every night, no exceptions.

When dinner was over, dishes had to be washed and put away. Then the girls needed their baths. By the time I tucked them into bed at eight, I could barely keep my eyes open let alone make any sort of sense of my homework.

If I hadn't already grown up, playing the role of a parent sure moved me along toward adult responsibilities.

For their fifteenth wedding anniversary, Allen and Lorain planned a trip away for a weekend at a resort in the Ozarks. The girls went to a local relative, and I went to stay with one of Allen and Lorain's friends.

The moment I walked into Pam's house, I knew why they'd chosen her. She was a drunk, the kind that drops fully clothed after their last drink. I guess you can't cry for help to someone who looked for her scotch when the glass was right in her hand.

Despite her obvious addiction, I welcomed the chance to stay at Pam's for a few days. At least I was temporarily out of harm's reach.

Pam was unique in my limited experience. She was painfully thin, had a "well-used" appearance that matched a description I'd heard one day on TV, and was somewhere between forty and sixty. Her skin color was spray-on tan deep orange-gold, a failed attempt to hide the constellation of liver spots on her body. Heavy lines creased her face like an old leather purse baked in the sun. And her voice was gravelly from burning through most of a pack of smokes with every tall glass of whiskey. From another room, she sounded like a man.

The thing about someone who's drunk, they aren't responsible for the things they say—Jim Beam does the talking.

"You know your foster dad ... he's a queer, don't you?" Pam brought the glass of bourbon up, rattled the ice, and took a sip.

I happened to be eating a bologna sandwich for breakfast, and I stopped in the middle of my chew. *What did she just say?*

"Yeah, the reason they have you and the girls, well ... they can't have kids." Pausing from her drink, she lit another cigarette, even as the cloud from the preceding one still hung in the air.

I don't know why, but I didn't say a word. I just listened. And I bet if I let her, she would tell me who killed Kennedy if she didn't pass out first.

"Can't have kids ... 'cause, well, he's got HIV."

Nothing on my plate was appetizing anymore. The meat in my half-eaten sandwich curled in the acrid air, and my stomach turned in nausea as Pam's vindictive rant about Allen picked up steam. *She* didn't like him much either.

Allen had contracted HIV from a homosexual relationship in college. Then, when he was a youth pastor at a church, he grew a little too fond of a young boy and tried to entice him into a sexual encounter. Wisely, the boy ran home to his parents, who in turn ran to the church board. End of the line for Allen. They stripped him of his ministerial license, and the family got a restraining order against him.

Now it all began to make sense. *I* was a teenage boy, and I must have reminded him of his past, a past he so desperately wanted to hide. But why in the world had the foster system let him be a parent? I concluded they must not have known—or worse, they didn't care.

I carried the secrets that Pam freely blabbed that day with me for as long as I could, but all secrets eventually find their way into daylight.

There was a trade show coming up in Nashville, and the Bochner's were going to set up a booth for their shop there. Allen and I were in the garage one weekend, working with various pieces of lumber to make the required display units. I was holding down a pair of 1x2s as Allen ran the circular saw across them. The blade jammed and kicked back one of the pieces. A piece of splintered wood tore across his knuckles.

"Urrgh," he exhaled. "Run and get me a paper towel, quick."

I took off as told and returned with a sheet of Bounty.

Before I handed him the makeshift bandage, I froze. He had suffered more than just a nick. A piece of flesh was peeled back from his fingers, and blood ran down his arm. HIV-infected blood.

My hesitation, and probably the look in my eyes, tipped my hand. I tried to hide my fear, but Allen's eyes sparked with anger, and he rushed me.

"Who told you?" he screamed. He wrapped his good hand around my throat and shoved me against the garage wall so hard my feet nearly left the concrete floor.

"I don't … know wha' … you're talking … abou'," I gasped for air as red fog colored the corners of my vision.

With his hand still clenched around my neck, Allen leaned down and grabbed the shattered piece of wood.

Thwaccckkk! He slammed the board into the side of my head and let me go. I dropped to the ground, dazed—half from asphyxiation and half from—

Thud! One of his boots drove into my side, and I curled into a fetal position.

"You should learn to mind your own business, you little—"

My ears were ringing so loudly I barely heard him, but I saw the board descending again.

I never felt it connect. My unconscious body lay sprawled out on the sawdust-covered garage floor.

From that event, I knew with detached clarity that someday—if no one stepped in or if I didn't take matters into my own hands—Allen, my foster *dad*, was going to kill me.

Nor was there any uncertainty I was trapped in hell.

The big question was, could anyone get me out?

11

"I'LL KILL YOU"

There is no hole so deep or so dark from which God cannot pull you out! God was there, continually by my side, yet seemingly silent. As painful as that time of anguish was, I was going to have to wait for the time he'd come to my rescue.

One day.

My hole—this deceptively dark house—was not too deep or too dark.

God would come through for me one day.

⟶⟶

Near the end of my eighth-grade year, Allen took the abuse to the next level. His father had been an officer in the US Navy during the Vietnam War, his field of expertise: psychological warfare. That's a fancy way of saying he knew how to mess with someone's mind.

We all have our breaking point; Mr. Bochner's job was to find it. Somehow, perhaps by sociopathic idolization of his father's skill set, Allen picked up a few of his father's techniques and began using them on me.

As usual when there are extra mouths to feed, money became tight. Allen found a part-time job on the second shift at a parcel warehouse across town. Most days he'd rush home from his daytime job with the girls in tow, fly through the house changing his clothes and grabbing a bite to eat, then head out the door for job number two, leaving me in charge of the girls until Lorain came home from the shop.

When he returned home past midnight, he found inventive ways of blowing off steam. The bedroom light came on, and I woke to the blinding light and a hand gripping the collar of my sleep shirt.

"Get up and come with me."

I knew by now to obey—no question asked and with no hesitation.

A dining chair sat facing him, across from his recliner. His grim expression meant *sit*. I took my place in the chair and tried to keep my chin up and my eyes open. I knew better than to close my eyes or turn my back to this man.

"What'd you do today at school?" His voice was neutral as he sat eating leftovers from the fridge.

I was tired and confused … exhausted by the long days. My brain couldn't find the answer to his inquisition.

"Umm … I don't remember." My head dropped, and I jerked it up, trying to stay awake.

"Don't remember?" His eyes narrowed. "Are you stupid, or just don't pay attention?"

"Sorry, I just don't remember, I guess." My head dropped again, chin to chest as my eyelids closed.

Wham! His fist pounded against the side of my face, shocking me back to consciousness. "Maybe this'll motivate you to pay attention."

I sat up fully and faced him. The side of my head throbbed, and fear twisted my insides.

"You can go back to sleep when I tell you!" Allen put his face inches away from mine. "This will teach you. You are weak and stupid, Levi. You need discipline."

He was the only one who believed his toxic motivational speech. Those nights happened often, more often than I'd like to admit, let alone think about.

When bruises started showing on my face, he changed to less noticeable methods of motivation. He began keeping a ruler next to his recliner for those nights. If I answered wrong or nodded off, I'd receive a harsh swat across the chest from the foot-long piece of wood.

Sometimes he'd fill a tote he found in the garage with ice-cold tap water, and it was just big enough to fit both my feet into the water. His rule was to keep one foot in the water at all times or suffer something worse. This left my feet in freezing agony as I alternated one foot in while the other warmed up. Very smart, because this never left any lasting signs of abuse.

That's all Allen was to me now: pain. He was a tyrant, and his times of torture would last for an hour or more before he'd finally send me off to bed. I wish his reign of oppression had ended with those nighttime sessions.

If I threw food away, even souring, moldy leftovers in the refrigerator, he would dig them out and make me eat them while he watched. There were even plenty of nights that, instead of his game of questions, he would sneak into my room and quietly ransack it, pulling drawers of clothes out of the chest, upending their contents on the floor and ripping my wardrobe from the closet. Obviously, I woke during these episodes, and I wasn't allowed to go back to sleep until I had put everything back perfectly.

When I absentmindedly put a piece of recycling into the trash, he would upend the can of garbage in my bed and demand I sleep with it: dog poop, coffee grinds, baby diapers, and all. It was his way of teaching me to pay attention. His favorite seemed to be to sneak into my room while I was sleeping, then punch or kick me underneath the blankets as many times as he could before I woke up and pushed him off with a scream that woke everyone in the house.

In response to the abuse, I checked out. I really didn't want to know what was going on around me anymore, and I began to long for the day that this would end—somehow.

My grades dropped so much that the first semester of my freshman year I received Fs in all of my classes. Allen got my report card and took me out of school early. When we pulled into the driveway I could tell by his silence that he had something sinister up his sleeve. We quietly walked into the house—no belittling and no mind games.

He pointed down the hall. "Go wait in your room until I say otherwise!"

I did as told.

A few minutes later, Allen came into my room, grabbed a handful of my shirt, and threw me onto the floor on my back. He straddled me, one hand working to unclasp my belt buckle. It wasn't hard to read his intent.

"You are going to do what I want you to, you understand?" his voice whispered in my ear.

I might never have fought back before, despite my strength being almost equal to his, but I wasn't going to have *this*.

"*G-et … o-ff … m-e!*" I growled, despite having one of his hands wrapped around my throat. Allen tried his best to overpower me. He leaned in close, close enough—

I butted my head into his nose.

Allen reeled back, blood streaming down his face. Taking advantage of his painful distraction, I squirmed from under him, brought both feet to his chest, and catapulted him off me. He flew back and his head crashed against the window, shattering the glass and showering him with fragments as he collapsed to the floor. He was dazed but still tried to stand. I couldn't let him get up. Not again. I had to finish this.

I sprang up, grabbed the lamp from my nightstand, and slammed my makeshift Louisville Slugger into the side of his head.

"You ever … try that again … I will kill you!" I huffed, half in an adrenaline rush, half trying to catch my breath.

Allen lay on his side for a moment, murmuring. Even as blood gushed from his nose and many cuts on his head, he tried to stand. I wasn't sticking around so I rushed out of the house, vaulted over the porch railing, and took off in a frenzied sprint down the street, zigzagging through the subdivision.

I wasn't going back. Not there, and not to *him*. Not ever again.

⌁

I had only been on the run for a few hours before the cops caught me. I was cuffed, then transported back to the station on the hard plastic seat of the police cruiser.

Allen had gone to the ER to have his wounds treated, which required stitches, liberal applications of disinfectant, and antibiotics for his crippled immune system. His wounds were enough evidence to lock me up—those coupled with a neighbor's testimony who'd been checking his mailbox when he heard the window break, followed by my scream of "I will kill you." And he'd seen me fleeing the house on foot.

I wasn't given the opportunity to tell my side of the story. Besides, who was going to believe a "troubled foster kid" anyway?

The authorities kept me locked up for almost two weeks while the courts figured out how to deal with me. My foster parents never came to claim me, but I have to admit I was somewhat grateful for that. Allen was the last person I wanted to see, and Lorain had rarely stood against his anger. Finally, I was informed of the court decision by my appointed public defender: I would spend ninety days in a juvenile rehabilitation facility called Ozanam.

⁓⁓

Ozanam, or "Oz," as we kids called it, was a facility where juvenile boys—most of whom were part of the state system already—could be "socially rehabilitated."

I guess that's a politically correct way of saying tame a wild animal, because that's what it felt like was happening. In the court's eyes we were wild and unsafe for domestic living. And like every other kid in Oz, I felt it unjust that I was there. I was, after all, innocent. Except no one wanted to hear it. No one cared.

Ozanam sat right outside the city limits of Kansas City, and its buildings sprawled over a dozen acres. Despite its venerable reputation as a behavioral home, it was anything but a home. It was a glorified low-security juvenile prison.

While only locked up at night in my private room, I couldn't go anywhere on campus unless given permission and under strict supervision. There were multiple buildings on the campus: a school, a gymnasium, two dormitories, a dining facility located on the bottom floor of one of the dormitories, and a chapel. There was also an administration building, but it was always securely locked. We were never allowed in or near it.

One of the dormitories was higher security and was a standalone building in the center of the campus. The dining hall was on the ground floor, making it easy for the guards to manage the high-risk residents.

The other dormitory, named Southwest, had two floors with two halls of rooms located off a central staff control room that had visible access and command over both halls. This hall, my temporary home, held the short-term residents, all of us serving a mandatory ninety days.

Despite the cozy words of *halls, home,* and *residents,* it was a jail. The buildings had cold, sterile concrete floors, and the bathrooms were locker-room style: open showers and exposed toilets. No privacy.

Each hall held ten boys, five rooms on each side of the hall.

Our rooms were ten-by-ten concrete bunkers with thin Berber carpet over the cold cement floors. The walls were painted baby blue, a color, I learned later, psychologically associated with suppressing aggression. A heavy oak door with a small Plexiglas viewing port was the only way in and out of the room, and the only other light fought its way through a window secured on both sides by an industrial-strength steel contraption of mesh and wire. It wasn't pretty to look at, and it served as a reminder that if you wanted out of this place, you were going to have to get out the *right* way: on foot with the proper walking papers—proof that you had learned your lesson the hard way.

The only furniture in the room was a steel-framed bed bolted to the floor, topped off with a mattress barely deep enough to keep your backside from being imprinted by the perforated steel frame underneath.

The bed was located close to a piece of laminate counter cemented into the concrete wall. By sitting on the bed, you could use the countertop for a desk. Cinder block half-height walls with a steel rod across the top served as a closet.

This was a lonely place, as it was intended; a place to leave you alone with your thoughts, alone to torment yourself and to contemplate the failure you had become.

Then again, at least I was safe. These locks and walls worked both ways. In here Allen couldn't get to me.

And then I met a man I would never have thought to ask for. Someone you could call a hero. Yes, he was a hero to me and to my wounded heart.

⚋⚋⚋

Mr. Redding was a man of myths and legends, and he turned out to be the one bright spot of this depressing facility.

To help us residents rehabilitate more effectively, we were given a caseworker, someone to help us process the mental side of our situations.

My stomach was in knots the day I arrived. After a plainclothes corrections officer checked me in and state-issued forms were stamped and signed, I was led back to my room. The lock tumblers fell into place in the secured door. The world continued somewhere beyond the tangled mesh of the steel-covered window, but it did so without me. I thought of the irony of this room and my situation. I was the victim, yet I was the one punished, locked up. Everything about this moment symbolized my life.

Suddenly I heard something decidedly out of place: someone humming a tune. The sound drew closer and closer until it stopped outside my door, followed by the distinct rap of knuckles against the wooden barricade. An electronic buzz reverberated and the door swung open, revealing a brown-haired, spectacled man standing in the entry.

"You must be Levi, that is unless they've locked up the wrong kid again, which always happens around here." He shot a shifty smile my way. "Tell you what, hop up and come with me. I'll break you out of this joint!"

I held my breath in bewilderment, but got up, grabbed my jacket and duffle, and approached him. "Really, man? You serious?" I wasn't wasting any time.

The man chuckled. "Of course … *NOT!*" He smiled even as I cringed at the old, yet still cruel joke. "I'm just kidding with you. Why would I be serious? You're stuck here for the ninety, Levi, so why don't you put your stuff down and come with me. Let's make the most of our time together."

I fought back tears at his jesting, even though I could tell he didn't mean it maliciously. Yet what he'd offered was all I really wanted in life: someone to take me away.

This was Mr. Redding.

Comical and wise, this middle-aged man always knew what to say to make me laugh. He walked with a swagger that looked kind of ridiculous, but he used it to break down the impenetrable walls we put up. And it was worth all the street cred money could buy. I guess he was the perfect man for this job, and everybody in Ozanam wanted him as his caseworker. I was one of the lucky ones.

He looked out for you and cared as if you were his own. To him, everything about us made sense, and it motivated him to help us get past the pain and the anger, and then lead us to hope. We were just hurting kids, acting out from a lifetime of mistrust. He didn't care that our hearts were hardened to the world around us or that the system saw us as untamed delinquents.

Nor did it matter that there were a couple of decades between his age and ours; we hung on almost every word he spoke, even when he was poking fun at our expense or at his own. Mr. Redding meant the world to me.

⁓

Each day of my incarceration, Mr. Redding came for me, and the two of us would head to his office in the admin building. For an hour we would sit and talk, beginning with juvenile banter and jesting while we snacked on the ever-present treats he kept on his desk. He'd eventually turn the conversation to what mattered most to him: the crud in my life.

Mr. Redding coaxed me to open up and talk about the very things I didn't want to think about, let alone talk about. In the hours he and I spent together drudging through the depths of my hurt, he helped me know more about myself than I thought possible.

This man became a treasured friend. He didn't abuse, he didn't judge—he just loved.

His philosophy was that life wasn't fair, it was fallen. You couldn't make others accept you, and you sure couldn't make them love you. And if you were going to make it in this cold, cruel world, you had to roll with the punches and have a little thing called faith.

Or hope. Or love.

I can't remember if it was one of the three or all of them together.

Anyhow, it was amazing what a little empathy could do for an embattled soul. Mr. Redding was the only one in this world who "got" me, and God used him to save my life.

A few days before my ninety was up, Mr. Redding appealed to the foster-care system to put me in a different home—anywhere—just as long as it wasn't with the Bochners.

As usual, his request fell on deaf ears.

I returned to the real world in time to finish the last quarter of my freshman year. Mr. Redding followed my transition back to society every step of the way, and he came to meet with me once a week at my foster parents' house. It was his way of keeping me safe and the situation with Allen in check.

When the school year finished and summer began, my probationary period was coming to an end. Per the courts, Mr. Redding would stop coming out to the house.

Our last evening together, we stood on the back deck overlooking the pool as the sun set.

"You know, I am going to miss your stubborn obstinance, young man," he joked as he shifted his soda to the other hand and put his arm around my shoulder.

"Yeah?" I smiled. "I might just miss you, too. Or maybe not!"

We both stood there laughing.

The time came for him to go, and the two of us walked through the house, past my foster parents sitting pleasantly in the living room watching some TV show with the girls, and out to the road where his pickup was parked.

Mr. Redding fumbled his keys. He choked up, blinking rapidly as we faced each other for the last time.

"Kid, with your stubbornness, you'll do just fine in life!" He gave me a bear hug, smiled, jumped in his truck, and waved good-bye in the rearview mirror. Like a hero riding off into the sunset.

I watched as his truck disappeared into the twilight, the taillights blurring in my wet eyes. A few minutes passed before I wiped my face and turned back to the house—the Bochner house. Although my stomach contracted to a hard rock, I knew I had to go inside.

I entered as quietly as possible and made a beeline to the bathroom to unload all the soda Mr. Redding and I had consumed on the deck. I had no sooner started my business when I heard a funny thudding sound in the kitchen and then in the hall. My brain had barely processed the noise as footsteps when—*crash!*

The bathroom door flattened against the wall in a shower of splinters. Allen grabbed me by the back of the neck, lifted me into the air, and slammed me to the floor. He pummeled my face several times, then pinned me with a knee on my throat.

"No! If you ever do that again, *I'll* kill *you!*" he spewed, repeating my last words to him before I was sent to Ozanam. "You hear me?" he swore, "*I'll* kill *you!*"

Lorain ran to my rescue, screeching, "Stop it, Allen! Get control of yourself! Stop it!"

Allen stood, his face twisted with maniacal glee, and I wondered for a moment if he'd resume the beating—perhaps this time including Lorain. But he scoffed at us and left the room.

Lorain looked at me, and I saw her strained expression release, shrinking back to her comfort zone of denial. She said nothing as she turned her back and returned to wherever she had come from.

I stood, shaking with adrenaline and fear. My brain didn't want to work right, and I felt woozy—like one of those blackouts was coming.

God, please … no … not this again. Not this again!

Blood streamed from my nose and dripped down the front of my shirt, and I paused at the reflection in the mirror. My nose was swollen. Broken.

I reached for the box of tissues on the end of the counter, but stopped when I noticed a framed piece of art of what appeared to be a poem hanging above the toilet. It hadn't been there when I was in this bathroom before.

I stared at the words scribed onto the painting. Words I will never forget.

12

EYE OF
THE STORM

Signs.

Little reminders along the way that someone, somewhere, knows exactly where you are. That he hasn't forgotten about you, he hasn't given up on you or passed you by, and that he doesn't plan on leaving you there to stay.

Divine ways that this someone lets you know that everything is going to be okay.

~~~

As I pulled out a wad of tissues and pressed them gently against my nose, I was captivated by this plaque, graced by the peaceful seaside shoreline in the picture and the words etched on its cracked paint. I don't know how it came to hang on the wall, but from that day on I would read it habitually, as if the hand of God had written it and placed it there just for me.

The poem inscribed on the painting was called "Footprints in the Sand."

One night I dreamed I was walking along the beach with God.
Many scenes from my life flashed across the sky.
In each scene I noticed footprints in the sand. Sometimes there were two sets of footprints, other times there was one only.
This bothered me because I noticed that during the hardest times of my life, when I was suffering from anguish, sorrow, or defeat, I could see only one set of footprints, so I said to God, "You promised me God, that if I followed you, you would walk with me always. But I have noticed that during the most trying

periods of my life there has only been one set of footprints in the sand. Why, when I needed you most, have you not been there for me?"

God replied, "The years when you have seen only one set of footprints, my child, is when I carried you."

Who would hang such a poem in a house where God clearly did not dwell? But that trivial question didn't matter, because this someone, God, wanted me to know I wasn't alone.

I had naively thought the footprints in my life were my own, but the poem's meaning gave me pause. It said I wasn't forgotten, even in this house where violence and hurt lurked around every corner.

And he wasn't going to leave me here.

―――

The mess of my life continued through the summer and into the fall semester. On the second day of my sophomore year, a group of us exited the school bus when it dropped us off near home. I always tried to squeeze out a few minutes of social time before I had to run into the house for my daily phone call to Allen.

The middle school bus came barreling down the road as it always did, moments behind ours. It stopped and the door opened.

Bradley got off, eyeballing us warily. Despite his best efforts to fit in, he was stereotypically nerdy. Small, a bit overweight, and plagued by a strong stutter, Bradley had grown used to most kids ignoring or making fun of him. But he was just being *him*. Besides, who was I to judge? You kidding me?

I liked the kid.

Bradley had wealthy parents who tried in all the wrong ways to help him make friends. They'd give him a wad of cash each week to take to school so he could buy a soda or candy for any kid who would sit with him at lunch or play with him at recess. It never worked, and I felt a little sorry for him.

That day at our bus stop, the crowd of kids had mostly scattered by the time Bradley got off, and he immediately spotted Thomas and me.

"Oh, man!" Thomas whined, thumping me in the shoulder to get my attention. "Bradley's coming."

Thomas, a junior, was the neighborhood enforcer—or at least that's what *he* thought. Really, he was a bully. He often made cruel fun of everyone, and I had a hard time tolerating him. He, too, grew up in a messed-up home, with several siblings under one roof, an alcoholic mom, and her live-in boyfriend. The boyfriend was a lowlife and on warm days could often be heard swearing at something out on the driveway under his rusty El Camino.

Thomas's mom seemed skittish around the boyfriend, and I knew firsthand what that meant—she was getting wailed on. Thomas probably was too, though I never saw bruises. But his silly bravado seemed like a cover.

Bradley made his way over to us and stopped, shifting the weight of his schoolbook-laden backpack to the other shoulder.

"Hey, guys." Sweat beaded on his forehead from nervousness. "I st-t-ill have the hundr-d dollar-s my fo-k's gave me this week. Y'all wann-a come play Plays-station-n wit- me? I'll ggi-ve you bo-th half?"

Inwardly I shook my head at Bradley's pathetic plea, but Thomas's reaction was to grab the straps of Bradley's backpack and jerk him around.

"Nobody wants to play with you, you stuttering twerp." Thomas reached inside his jean shorts and pulled out a switchblade, snapping it open with a noticeable *flick*. He brandished the blade in front of Bradley. The boy began to shake, tears filled his eyes, and a dark spot formed on the front of his pants. A distinct odor of urine rose from an expanding yellow puddle at his feet.

"Thomas, please don't hurt me." Bradley squirmed in Thomas's grasp as he cried. "You can have all the money, and what I get next week too!"

I'd had enough of this bullying in my own life to last a lifetime.

"Thomas! Get off him. Now!" I barked, closing the distance between us.

Thomas shoved Bradley away and spun, facing me with his weapon.

"You gonna make me?"

Without even thinking, I leaned back and kicked the knife out of his hand with a speed I didn't even know I possessed. It was just instinct.

In a brief millisecond, Thomas's eyes widened in disbelief, then he took off running. I chased him between two houses, past swing sets and bicycles strewn behind homes, and down the hill to his house on the next street over. He had just jumped onto his backyard fence when I caught up with him.

Thomas was almost over the top when I grabbed the back of his pants and tugged on his belt, sending him flailing backward.

While he was still in free fall, I balled my fist and punched him in the head. Thomas landed in a heap. Although disoriented, he tried to stand and fight back. Before he could get his balance, I wrapped my hands around the back of his head and jerked it down toward my rising knee. Thomas dropped into a pile and I kicked him.

"What is wrong with you?" I screamed, cursing at him as I kicked his motionless body. I drove my foot into his head again. "Pick on someone who can fight back."

"Stop it!" A voice squealed from the direction of his house, stopping my attack.

Oh man.

It was Thomas's mom, and she was running at me with a foot-long kitchen knife. I turned my gaze from her and kicked Thomas one more time, then I spit on him and took off in full sprint back to my house before she could get to me.

After I rushed into the house and locked the door, I sat on the bottom of the stairs to the second floor and tried to catch my breath. I was late, very late, for my call to Allen. How was I going to explain this?

My fingers shook as I dialed Allen's work line.

"You're seven minutes late, Levi. Why?" He never bothered with pleasantries.

"I ... got ... in a ... fight," I panted. *Click* ... and the annoying dial tone.

Just as I hung up the phone, a cop car pulled up with lights silently flashing on our driveway. Two officers got out, one with his hand on his holstered firearm. Two more squad cars braked to a stop at the curb.

I hung my head as I looked out the front window, sighed, and reached for the lock to open the door.

For over an hour I sat cuffed in the backseat of the cruiser while Thomas's mom stood nearby telling one of the officers what she saw. Allen, having left work earlier than normal—most likely the moment he hung up the phone—stood talking to the other cop. An icy look in his eyes sent its corresponding shiver through me. This wouldn't end well.

When the police had what they needed, Allen went inside, the cops climbed inside the car with me, and we drove away.

I spent the next few nights at the county jail, a déjà vu reality to my time before. Thomas spent two nights at the hospital. By my hand he had suffered a broken nose, broken jaw, a severe concussion, and a split in his right cheek that required several stitches. He'd been unconscious when the paramedics got to him. One of the treating doctors told the police that even one more blow could have killed him.

Even though Thomas's family wasn't pressing charges, the justice system wasn't going to let me off the hook. I had almost killed someone. When my hearing came up, the judge told me I had "exceeded the right to defend" myself. For that I was going back to Ozanam for twelve to twenty-four months.

Time is not your friend—not when you are locked away. It begins to crawl by. A week feels like a month, a month like a year. Each day is a new sentencing all its own, and if you let it, it will eat away your sanity.

Back at Ozanam, I had the reunion I wished was under different circumstances. Mr. Redding had my case again. Like true friends, we picked up where we left off—well, minus me being free on the outside.

About six months in, Mr. Redding took it upon himself to plead my case to the authorities and the foster-care system, saying I had been rehabilitated and deserved to go home—to a different home.

Like before, his voice and wisdom were ignored. His act of

advocacy backfired, and I was pulled from his supervision and given to another caseworker. The Bochners had a hand in that decision, and now I was given to Ms. McClure.

Losing Mr. Redding was disheartening, and I shut down again. Maybe it was partly in protest to the injustice, but it was more because I lost the only person to ever understand me. He understood *life*. I needed his wisdom.

<hr/>

Ozanam had a chapel on its grounds, an old stone and brick building with mosaic stained-glass windows and old antique red velvet upholstered pews. It was barely big enough to hold two dozen people, and the chapel was the eldest building on the campus, going back to when Ozanam first bought the land in the 1930s. Every other structure had been rebuilt for security improvements. But not the chapel. She stood untouched, a time capsule of the past.

The man responsible for holding down the fort was Chaplain Wes, or "Chap" to those who knew him well. Wes was middle-aged, tall and muscular, and had spiked hair. What really set him off from the other adults at Oz were his sleeve tattoos on both arms and the phrase *Live Free* inked in Old English across his knuckles.

Wes was a reformed motorcycle thug. A scar ran along his left cheekbone as testament to his old life. He said he'd gotten it from "an old drunken indiscretion," a memento of a bar fight a decade prior. He definitely wasn't your stereotypical pastor.

And Wes was just the man to talk to a bunch of juvenile delinquents about God.

Tuesday nights, Chaplain Wes would swing by each dorm and invite us to join him in the chapel for a few hours. He had stiff competition, though, since that was during our nightly TV time and also the one night we could use the phone to touch the outside world. Few accepted his offer.

My first go around at Oz, I never went to chapel. I didn't care. But this time I found the opportunity to get out of the dorm as appealing as a mini vacation. Why not? This place would be my home for the next two years.

Most of our nights together, two or three of us gathered in the old building. We'd watch some video about the Bible or just sit and shoot the breeze, listening to Chap tell stories about his life and how God had gotten hold of him.

I loved to lean back on the old creaky pew and watch the moonlight filter through the stained glass onto our group. The ancient smell of the building enriched the experience, far different from the sterile Clorox odor in the dorms.

For a few hours on those nights—and for the first time in my life—I felt *free*.

In the serenity of that chapel, I found a home.

⎯⎯⎯

A night came when Chaplain Wes came by and I was the only boy to join him. Wes and I walked through the arched door of the chapel, then he motioned with the tilt of his head for us to go into his office off to the side.

"This should do," he said, flicking on the lights in the small room. "Definitely easier on the backside than the ole pews!" Wes waved me to an old sofa that looked like it had been a bed to some hobo back in its day. He plopped down into the oversized leather chair behind his desk and leaned forward, resting his tattooed arms on the desk. His eyes narrowed, and the corners of his mouth twitched as if he was about to smile.

"Kid, you up for a ride?"

"Sure, what did you have in mind, Chap?" I replied, going along with his playful banter. He and I both knew I couldn't leave for a joyride.

Wes leaned to one side and opened the mini fridge under his desk. He set a pair of Dr. Peppers on the desk, then tossed out a bag of chilled M&Ms.

"Dang, man!" My eyes widened at the abundance of sugar before us. "Now that's a stash! You been holding out this whole time?"

"Nah, jus' saving them for a special occasion. It's going to be a long night." The grin that had threatened before now spread across his face.

"I take it we're not going back to the dorm anytime soon?"

Wes shook his head. "I've got free reign of this place. I can bend the rules a bit if I like." He cracked open one of the DPs and handed it to me. "Besides, you and me need to have a man-to-man talk, if you feel me?"

I grabbed the soda and tried to play nonchalant. "About what?" I suspected where he was going with this—he was a man who seized every opportunity. Still, I was captivated by such a wide and winning smile on a man who looked like the leader of a biker gang.

"Levi, why are you here?" He leaned back in his chair and thunked a steel-toe boot onto the desk. "Why are you *really* here?"

Great, here we go. Not this whole song and dance again. "Man, I talk about this in therapy all the time with Ms. McClure." I stood from my seat. "I'd rather just go back to the dorm now."

Wes laughed at my posturing. "Sit your hide down, kid. You ain't going back until I take you back." He took a swig of soda and met my eye. "Understood?"

"You're just going to hold me hostage then?" I threw back at him, suddenly angry, even though I knew he wasn't being malicious.

"Son," his tone became serious, "you're already a hostage!"

"Because I'm in here? Chap, man, I'll do my time, then leave this place. Who knows, by then maybe I'll be too old for the foster system and I can leave all that trouble behind me. This is temporary."

"That's true." Wes removed his foot from the desk and tore open the bag of chocolates. "One problem with that thought: Ozanam isn't what holds you captive—it's in your heart."

I scoffed at his words. "How is that?"

Wes picked out a couple of M&Ms and flipped them into his mouth. "In what you think about God." His response was as natural as breathing to him. To me, it was untouched territory.

God was the *last* person I wanted to talk about. I wasn't going to let Wes take the high ground on this, so I reached my hand for some candy and sat back, trying to play it cool.

But a verbal wrestling match about God with Chaplain Wes would leave you with your prideful tail tucked between your legs.

"Let me ask you something. What if everything you thought about God ... was wrong." His words were a right hook to my line of thinking. I had never heard that question before. He continued, "What if everything *we* thought about God is wrong? *All* of us."

My expression narrowed to a squint as my brain cramped at what he said.

"Sometimes we can't see the forest for the trees. That's cliché, but still true. The trees are all the crud in our lives that keep us from seeing God." Wes leaned back in his chair and kicked his feet up onto the desk again. "I mean, look at the world today—even the church. Can we confidently say we know who God is?"

His words were a Rubik's Cube, and I didn't know how to solve it. "Huh, Chap, I don't follow. You trying to be Yoda or something?"

"Well, follow *this* for a moment: God is love—pure, limitless, ever-forgiving, all-consuming love, right? Yet look at us ... the world around us. Can we dare to say we *know* God? I think if we really knew God and understood him, there would be a lot more love and a lot less hate."

I knew from my sessions with Ms. McClure that anger and hate were closely related, and it had been my overwhelming anger at Thomas that landed me here. But I also knew hate. That's what I felt for Allen Bochner. It wasn't love, that was for sure. And I knew those emotions were far from any picture of God I still carried. But I hadn't let them go.

"I guess you're right," I said, still chewing it around in my head. "I never thought of it like that."

"I don't think many people have. Oh, they might *say* they have, but talk is cheap. The way we live life proves our beliefs."

I thought again of Thomas's broken jaw and nose, the blood, his glassy eyes as I kicked him again and again. For the first time, I felt shame for what I'd done. Not for sticking up for Bradley, but for my anger and hate. In some ways, what I'd done to Thomas was exactly what Allen Bochner did to me. If there was one thing in life I didn't aspire to, it was modeling my life after Allen.

Wes shifted, and the old leather squeaked as he found a more comfortable position. "Levi, I've noticed when you come here to the chapel, you gaze around, almost like you're looking for something—or should I say *someone*. Are you looking for God?"

Wes saw through my seeming inattention at those times. The man was sharp.

"Just the forest for the trees, kid." He grinned again.

I shot him a look, as if to say I wasn't pleased with his playfulness.

"What?" He seemed innocently offended by my demeanor. "I'm being real with you. For real, can you see God in anything, everything around you?" Wes stood and made his way over to me and the empty spot on the couch where I'd sat down again.

Was he trying to imply that God was in my life ... in Ozanam? I gathered my thoughts as best I could before replying to a man I deeply respected. "Man, you have got to be kidding. God in this? In my life?" My words dripped with sarcasm at the very idea of that. "Do you know what I've been through? If you did you wouldn't be spouting off such trash."

He momentarily left the couch to get two more sodas out of the fridge.

"Levi, I started reading your file the day after we met," he said gently, and I felt the compassion in his words. "You have walked through more in sixteen years than any other kid I've known to cycle through this facility. I respect that, I get it ... I really do!" A tear welled in his eye. "Man, but what if you are missing everything?"

My own eyes started to blur. "Do you mean I'm missing a normal life?" A drop slid down my cheek, but its track burned, more pain than a tear. "Man, just 'cause you've read my past, doesn't mean you know my pain. Because if you did, you sure wouldn't be saying God was anywhere near this!" I put my head down and mumbled, "If he was, he wouldn't have let any of this happen."

Wes drew close to me, his voice a whisper. "Just the forest for the trees, Levi. How can God prove to you he is there for you if you have already made up your mind he isn't?"

My chest heaved, the beginning of a sobbing cry. "Uh ... he's God. He could think of *some* way."

"I know God wants to meet you in this, to prove he is there for you. But what does that have to look like for you to see it?"

"I don't really care at this point." Tears were flowing freely down my face.

"Levi," Wes said, leaning back into the old couch, "if you were stuck in a violent storm, say a hurricane, and there is no way you could get out of it, what would you do? Where would you go?"

I paused, thinking of his question while I swiped away the tears, glad we were off the *God* topic. "I dunno. Make my way to the eye of the hurricane, you know, where it's peaceful and stuff."

Wes jumped from the sofa and clapped his hands. "That's it, man! That's just it. This life is that storm—the hurricane—powerful, violent, and constantly churning. It's so much bigger than us, and if we let it, it will destroy us." Wes sat back down beside me, but he vibrated with excitement. "And God is the eye of the storm—peaceful, tranquil, ruling over all the storm—but he is *not* the storm."

I pictured that image: a powerful hurricane, dark and nasty, with lightning sizzling all around me. I imagined what it would be like sitting in a boat surrounded by massive waves, but me safe in the eye of the storm, peaceful as the sun shone upon me.

God—the eye of the storm.

But it still hurt. The tears flowing freely down my face were evidence of that. A nice picture didn't make *my* world go away.

"Why couldn't he just make the storm stop?" I sniffled a highlight to my words, and Wes handed me a tissue. He paused in contemplation to my question.

"I know this doesn't make any sense now, Levi, but in the Bible God says to a man who was going through unreal heartache of his own, 'Be still, and know that I am God.' Let's play a word game with that: if God is love like the Bible says elsewhere, take out the word *God* and put in *love*, and it would read, 'Be still and know that I am love.'"

I couldn't figure out where he was going with this. "Okay. But if God is love, why not just stop all of this … stop the storm?"

"Maybe he wants you to come to the eye of this storm, so you can be with him and know he is love."

I couldn't run from this anymore. I knew what Wes meant, and I began to cry harder than I had since my mother's death. "I jus' … want the … storm to … stop." I gulped for air between words.

Chaplain Wes scooted close to me and draped one of his bulky, ink-covered arms around my shoulder. "I know, man, I know. The storm isn't going to stop, though … it's life. This is a jacked-up world, and it's full of other people who we can't control." He finished his words and drew me to his chest in the strongest hug I'd ever had.

I was a sobbing mess in his arms, but it seemed his strength squeezed out a little of the pain.

"But I promise you, Levi, I have been there. Go to the eye of the storm. God wants to meet you there, *in this,* and prove to you he is love."

⁓

The eye of the storm. To the core of all that hurt. I had to go there. Question was, would I find what I was looking for? Would I find God? Would I find love?

13

THE LONGEST
OF DAYS

Thirteen months into my second tour of duty at Ozanam, I was sent home. I had proven to Mr. Redding, Ms. McClure, and the courts that I was rehabilitated and deserved release.

Mr. Redding and Ms. McClure both asked that I be sent to a different foster home.

Again, nothing happened.

I returned back to the Bochners', and to my high school, Riverview South, which was already two months into the school year. It was my junior year, and coming back to society was like hopping onto a treadmill already cranked up to full speed.

To help my transition back to South, as we called it, I was given a 504 Coordinator—Ms. Boyden. She was a guidance counselor specifically for kids with learning disabilities or behavioral problems, and she was given the task to keep those so labeled moving forward in high school. She and I met once a week for the rest of the school year, and she, in some ways, saved my life.

Ms. Boyden became like a mother to me, which seemed to come naturally to her, given that she had four kids of her own. From her hip, fun, and caring ways, you could never have guessed she was middle-aged.

She got to me immediately. Maybe it's because she resembled my mom a little: blonde hair, though hers was highlighted and streaked, up-to-date clothes, and a resilience that wouldn't take a load of bull from anyone—she was just what every kid with a tough upbringing needed. Just like my mom, Ms. Boyden kept me in line—kept *all* of us in line. And you could tell by the way she spoke to you, and listened, that you mattered to her.

For the first semester, I had to attend school in a segregated area of the building where the other behavioral kids had their classes. None of us were able to leave that section of the school unless given permission, and when it came time for our weekly meeting together, Ms. Boyden would send one of the school security guards to fetch me. Usually, it was Jon who came.

Jon was an awesome guy. Tall, black, and with some serious dreadlocks that draped to the middle of his back, he had been an artist for Disney before he burned out and needed a change of scenery. Even though he was about to hit thirty, he and I connected.

Jon was as wise as he was strong, and his gift for art didn't stop with drawings—which he could crank out in record speed. His friendship helped me transition back to regular life much more quickly.

Life outside of school hadn't changed over thirteen months. Allen's abuse fully resumed the week I returned from Ozanam. The dude was psycho.

Occasionally, one of my classmates or a teacher would ask about one of the marks on my face or arms. Sometimes words can't describe what one goes through, so I kept my mouth shut. Besides, if Mr. Redding couldn't fix it, no one else could.

One day I was in Ms. Boyden's office for our regular meeting, absently running my tongue over my swollen lip, a gift from a tyrant the night before. She opened her mouth to say something but stopped. I could tell by the look in her eyes she knew what had happened without even asking. She shot me a strange smile I hadn't seen before, as if to say, *I'll fix this.* Thankfully, the school bell rang, ending our awkward moment, and I zipped out of her office hoping to dodge any further inquiry.

But Ms. Boyden wasn't dumb, nor was she scared of a man who terrified me. The next day, Jon came to my class to pull me out, and I knew without being told where we were heading and why.

Jon, to his credit, *didn't* know and casually cracked jokes like he always did. Despite my misgivings about what was probably coming, I attempted sincere laughs. The look he gave me when we reached Ms. Boyden's office spoke my efforts had fallen short.

"See you later, Bro," he said solemnly.

"Later, man." I stuck out my hand and knocked knuckles, then sat down in the chair by the door as I always did.

"Hey, kiddo, don't get too comfy." Ms. Boyden logged off her computer, grabbed her keys and wallet, and came toward the door. "Why don't we go for a walk?"

As we strode down the hallway, I asked, "What's up? Is this about one of my classes or something?"

"Not today. Say, you hungry?" Her smile was always warm. "Never mind … when is a teenage boy *not* hungry? How about you follow me? My treat."

We walked past the cafeteria and turned the corner to the teachers' lounge. I sat down at one of the tables as she angled toward the vending machine before she sat down, offering me a soda and a couple of candy bars.

"Here you go. Hope it hits the spot. If you're still hungry afterward, there is more where that came from." Ms. Boyden smiled softly. "Hon, we're not here to talk about your grades. I need to talk to you about something far more important, if that's all right with you."

I had just ripped open the first candy bar, stopping before taking a bite. *Ms. Boyden, please don't go there. I know you care, but please … don't.*

"Levi, I know you haven't had many folks you could count on, let alone trust. So I'm going to be really bold, though, and ask you to trust me … Trust me in this." Ms. Boyden reached for the soda and cracked the seal for me. "You know I care, right?"

I nodded.

"I don't know how to ask it without just asking it. Is Allen hurting you?"

I was in a no-win situation.

"Ms. Boyden …" My eyes filled with tears. "I, uhh …"

She put her hand over mine and wrapped her arm around my shoulders.

"It's okay. It's okay." Her hand squeezed mine as I put my head down on the table and sobbed. "I promise you, this is all going to stop, and soon!"

Later, we sat in her office. Her maternal instincts weren't going to let me out of her sight until she fixed this. She made a phone call, and after a few moments, the school police officer came into the office and sat down beside me. I didn't have to say a word—Ms. Boyden said all that needed to be said, and for the rest of the afternoon the three of us met in her small, windowless office.

Officer Chapman was a street-smart cop who, after taking a bullet to the knee, chose the school position over a desk job. We weren't long into our conversation when he spoke up.

"I can't officially tell you this"—he shot a look to Ms. Boyden as if to say *nobody heard this from me*—"but you're seventeen, and according to state laws you can emancipate yourself. You'd need a lawyer, but you'd be free of your foster home and the system."

He might have said more, but then again, he never said anything to begin with, did he?

Only problem with his idea was, how could I hire a lawyer when I couldn't leave Allen's sight, let alone make money? The day ended, and Ms. Boyden walked me to the bus.

"Everything is going to be okay, kiddo. I promise." She wrapped her arms around me in a tight hug before I stepped onto the bus and left for home.

⁓⁓⁓

The next morning, which was a Friday, Allen remained at home instead of leaving for work.

"You're riding with me to school today, Levi," he said across the table as the girls and I ate breakfast.

When we got to the school, Allen led the way back to a conference room right outside the main office. One by one, each of my four teachers joined us. I was confused, being it was only six weeks into the second semester and too early to be talking about my grades.

And then Ms. Boyden walked in, followed immediately by Officer Chapman in street clothes. I almost puked all over the table as sweat began to saturate the palms of my hands. *No. What is she doing?*

My math teacher, Mr. Carver, who was the head wrestling coach and no wimp, spoke first.

"You know, Mr. Bochner, if there are problems in the home and Levi isn't safe, Officer Chapman here can see to it that he is placed in another home until he is eighteen."

Allen shot me a frosty glance before offering his response. "That's not necessary. He is perfectly fine, other than the scrapes he gets into with neighborhood kids from time to time. You do know he's been under treatment for assault and anger issues in a state facility?"

Ms. Boyden had had enough of the bull and leaned toward Allen. "Bochner, I can't speak for the others here, but if you expect me to believe that story for one moment, you are mistaken!" She wasn't scared of a confrontation. "I have come to see he is a very good kid. While he has had a troubled past, he is not the hoodlum many have painted him to be." She stood and looked at Officer Chapman. "I believe we are done here."

My teachers stood to leave the room, and Officer Chapman handed Allen his card. "Mr. Bochner, I'll see to it that the Division of Social Services will be putting Levi in a new home."

Allen turned away from him, almost ignoring what was said to him and by whom, and pinned me with a cold stare. "I guess the truth always comes out now, doesn't it?"

What in the world did he mean by that?

The room cleared, and I was the last one out, following Allen into the hall. He walked to the school's front door, keeping his back to me the whole time. As he reached the exit, he turned and shot me such a murderous look, a chill went down my spine. Then he pushed past the door and was gone.

I was left standing alone in the hall, my stomach roiling in acid.

That school day was the longest of my life.

⌘

A quarter past three. The bus roared away down the road as I stood in the wake of its diesel fumes looking at my front door. I knew I had to go inside and call him, but my gut told me Allen wasn't going to forget about this morning, *ever*. I sighed and headed for the house.

Inside, I picked up the phone. *Ringggg. Ringggg.* Silence. I could hear faint breathing at the other end, and the distant noises of the workplace beyond Allen's cubicle. My mouth dried up. I didn't know what to say. "Umm … so what chores did you want me to get done—"

"When I get home"—a sterile voice, his voice, interrupted me midsentence—"you are going to hurt in ways you have never hurt before!"

Click.

I knew at that moment it was over. He wasn't a man of hollow words. I sat on the edge of the bed thinking of how to work my way out of this one, what to say to him to get him to believe I hadn't said anything about what he did to me. And I knew that this day one of us was going to die. I was going to have to take his life, or he would probably take mine. Either way this was the end of the line for him and me.

I stared at the floor and wept. I didn't really want to spend the rest of my life locked up—not over a dirtbag like Allen. I was still weeping when I heard a soft voice speak.

You can't be hurt if you are not here. Leave, and don't look back. Come to me.

I raised my head and looked around. Did I just hear someone say something?

I wasn't sure what I had heard, but all of a sudden I had an idea: Leave. As in run away.

I shot from the edge of my bed and grabbed my backpack, quickly unzipped it, and dumped out my schoolbooks. I had to be swift if I was going to do this. Allen was the type to leave work just to come beat me, and he was probably on his way now.

In a mad dash, I darted through my room, grabbing a couple sets of clothes, my wallet, CD player, my stash of whatever food I had tucked away in my room, and the American flag hanging over the head of my bed, and I ran out the front door.

Not long after I had stepped off the school bus on February 2, 2001, my feet hit the pavement beyond my driveway. I tore away from the hellhole of my foster parents. I didn't look back, not that I wanted to. I had to follow wherever it was my feet would take me. Besides, anywhere was guaranteed to be better than this place.

I was running away.

14

ROUGHIN' IT

Run and don't look back! Sometimes it's exactly what we need to do. At seventeen years old, I was on the run. There wasn't time to look over my shoulder, as somewhere beyond the terror and confusion, I could have sworn I heard a Man call out to me: *Leave, and don't look back ... come to me!*

Regardless of whose voice it was or where it came from, he was right. I had to leave. Anywhere was better than here.

The afternoon sun was just beginning to give way to the night of winter. I had to move fast, putting as much distance as possible between the Bochner house and me.

I ran until my sides cramped with pain.

And then ran some more.

Before long, I had traversed the entire subdivision and made my way to a friend's house. I figured I could ask to use her phone. The only person I could think of calling was Officer Chapman. Maybe he could take me to the homeless shelter he mentioned, a place he said took in teen runaways. It was one of the things I wasn't supposed to have heard him say.

Jenna came to the door with a puzzled look on her face. "Levi, what are you doing here?" None of my friends had ever seen me outside of school.

I panted for air, my cheeks red from windburn. "I ... uhh ... Ca' ... I ple'e ... use ... your phone?"

Jenna invited me inside and gave me a warm cup of tea while I made my call—well, tried to, anyway. Officer Chapman wasn't answering his phone. Jenna's mom came home to a strange kid in her house. By now, Jenna was up to speed on the day's events, and she filled in her mom.

Debbie was a true mom and wasn't having me go to any teen homeless shelter. She offered for me to stay with them until I could get all of this sorted out.

Debbie, a divorcée, was a surrogate mom to all of Jenna's friends. With a gentle, endearing soul, her kindness often surprised many in this cold world. Debbie had taken many kids under her wings and loved them as if they were hers. And she loved to hug; you couldn't go by her without her telling you how awesome you were simply for being you.

That night, Debbie put out fresh sheets in the guest room and told me to call her house my home until I figured out how to get back on my feet.

⸺

I had run away from home on Friday, and I knew my foster parents would show up looking for me at school come Monday. So I stayed away from school that day. However, I couldn't skip school forever, and went back on Tuesday.

Jon intercepted me at my locker.

"Hey, man." Dread etched his face. "Sorry, brother, but you gots to come with me. Your foster dad is in the counseling office—just a heads-up."

Jon was a true friend, and he walked one step behind me, like he was my bodyguard.

"They were both here yesterday, too," he said as we reached Ms. Boyden's office door. We both knew what lay on the other side. "No worries, though. I got your back—believe that." Jon smiled. He was a big dude, and it was comforting to know he was on my side.

I took a deep breath, forced the knot in my throat back down, and shot him a smile before I stepped into the office.

The cramped room was overflowing. Ms. Boyden sat behind her desk with a look of determination on her face, and both Allen and

Lorain sat in the chairs across from the desk. Officer Chapman—in full police gear—stood next to Ms. Boyden. There was an extra chair next to Ms. Boyden, and Officer Chapman motioned me toward it.

Lorain began to cry as soon as I walked into the room. "How could you do this to us? We have been worried sick about you!"

Ms. Boyden shot a silent, sarcastic look, as if to say, *Oh, please!* Then she turned to me with another silent message: *Everything is going to be okay, kiddo. I promise!*

"You will come home tonight, Levi, or I will make sure you go back to Ozanam until you are twenty-one for violating your probation. You understand me?" Allen spoke, still possessed by his icy demeanor.

Officer Chapman ran his hands along his utility belt and cleared his throat, clearly irritated by my foster dad's presence. He moved a step closer to Allen and Lorain's seats.

"See, Mr. Bochner, that's just it. Levi doesn't have to return to your home," Officer Chapman declared. "There's this law in our country that gives a seventeen-year-old citizen the right to emancipate themselves. Now, I know you might not understand the meaning of that word, but I'll sum it up for you: it means Levi doesn't have to come back and, as the police, we don't consider him a runaway, nor will we make him go back. Oh, and as for your delusions of the law, he hasn't violated his probation in any way." Officer Chapman smiled. *Checkmate.* He was, after all, the only one in the room with a badge—and a gun.

It was over! I felt it deep inside my core. *It was over!*

I stood up and looked my foster dad square in the eye. It was the first time I wasn't afraid of him. "Allen, you're never going to see me again, let alone touch me. Now, if you will excuse me, I have to go to class."

I turned to Ms. Boyden, who was smiling in pride. *Way to go, kiddo; you faced your fears.* I mouthed thank you to her, smiled at Officer Chapman, and left the room without acknowledging Allen or Lorain.

⌇⌇⌇

Jenna and her mom were so hospitable, it didn't take long for me to see this as a home away from … well, it felt like a home. I was safe, I wasn't hungry, and best of all, I was *free.*

Jenna worked at the Sonic drive-in a short drive across town, and I took her up on an offer of a job. She was a year older, had a license and a car, and we rode to school and worked together each day. I was just glad to be able to start living what felt like a semi-normal life, even if I had no clue what I was going to do with myself tomorrow. Sonic was my first job, and I started putting away as much cash as I could to pay for the court fees to legally emancipate myself.

Then, at the end of March, just one paycheck away from having enough cash for my legal process, Jenna and I came home to a nightmare.

Debbie had been killed that afternoon in a car accident on her way home. Jenna and I sat numbly at the kitchen table as she talked with her dad on the phone. Silent tears dripped down her face. Her dad was coming from Oregon to pick her up and move her back with him after the funeral.

With Debbie's passing, I lost a friend, a loving place to stay, and someone who stood behind me as I went after my dreams. And Jenna lost her mom.

Jenna left with her dad the day after the funeral, so I quit my job at Sonic and embarked on foot for the teen homeless shelter. The setting sun drowned in a gray cloud as I walked across town, tears filling my eyes.

〜〰〜

I got to the shelter and checked in, but I had a surprise when they said I couldn't attend school while staying there. I'd have to drop out. The only help they offered was a roof over your head, three hot meals, a warm bed, and help getting your GED, if you wanted one. But no regular school attendance! I guess I was an exception to the type of teen they normally saw.

Drop out? I'm not doing that.

I started calling around to friends—what few I had—to see if they had any ideas. Lee, a buddy of mine, came through with an idea and a ride—his *actual* ride. A minivan was his big idea. Lee said I could sleep in the van on the driveway of his grandparents' house since staying inside wasn't an option. So that's what I did for the next two weeks until another buddy, Matt, had a better solution.

Matt's dad was a retired submarine captain and an avid outdoorsman. Matt also happened to live at the edge of the town, and behind his house stretched countless miles of woods. He thought, why be homeless when I could camp out behind his house? I was getting tired of the minivan's confined space, so it sounded good to me.

The spot we chose had already been cleared out; it was a place where he and others had gathered to party with other kids. A stream isolated the makeshift clearing in the heavily wooded area, and you had to cross the water on a fallen tree just to get to it.

That night, while his dad was off at a bar, Matt and I liberated a surplus of supplies from their garage and attic and took off for the woods. We constructed one formidable campsite, and this was where I'd call home for the time being.

The campsite had everything I needed: a propane cooking stove, a tank full of drinking-cooking water, a lean-to we built out of lumber from behind his house, and a good old fire pit. I kept a stash of military MREs in a chest next to my lean-to so raccoons and other creatures wouldn't steal them. Last, I draped the American flag I had along the back of my lean-to—until I got cold at night; then it came off and was used as an added layer to wrap up in.

It was my own little fort out in the wilderness.

I continued going to school, even through my homelessness, because I wanted to. Dropping out was never an option, not just because I was stubborn, but because most people assumed that in my circumstance I *would* drop out. It felt like I was being bet against, and I knew Allen wanted me to fail. So I just put my chin up and kept marching on.

A bus stop happened to be less than a mile away from my campground, and I would wake up early each morning, make sure the fire was out, and take off to catch my big yellow ride to school.

When I'd get to school, I would beeline to the locker room and take a shower, then head off to the cafeteria for a free meal.

After school, Matt, who attended a vocational school, would pick me up, and we'd ride together to his job at the Apple Market, a family-run grocery store where I was able to work sacking groceries.

The school year ended. I had stuck to it and made it through my junior year. Now it was time to rethink my strategy, because it was already miserably hot and humid in Kansas City. With no access to the school locker room, there wasn't enough Old Spice available to cover the endless body odor that came with living like a refugee.

I decided to go to the teen shelter now that the school year was over. Matt gave me a ride to the Apple Market so I could quit my job since the shelter didn't let anyone leave, then he dropped me off at my new residence.

I settled into the routine. The meals were good, and the air conditioning felt great during the hot summer. But the shelter was a roof over my head for only two weeks when I was told I would have to leave. Apparently the organization had to notify everyone's next of kin about who was staying under their roof. When they called my foster parents, they were threatened with a lawsuit if they continued to "aid a runaway."

Ah, good ol' Allen and Lorain.

Once again I was out on the street, thinking fast and watching my back. Now it was the norm, and I was getting used to it.

Over the next few weeks of summer, I drifted from one friend's house to another, couchsurfing. I was wise enough to know I didn't know too much in this world, but I did know one thing: camping in the woods, sleeping in a minivan, and couchsurfing all beat living at the Bochners'.

Until a friend came through in a way I never could have expected.

15

A MESSAGE FROM BRAZIL

Life seems to have this silent rule to play by: Watch the company you keep, the people you listen to, the places your heart longs to go. Because the company you keep ... will keep you.

⁓⁓⁓

Natalie was a girl I had struck up a friendship with after my second trip to Ozanam. Lively, with a spunky way about her, Natalie was hard not to notice—at least for me. She had choppy platinum hair, fiercely lit blue eyes, and a perfect smile. Everyone I knew thought she looked great. Except her.

When she looked in the mirror, she saw an ugly girl, an ugly, *fat* girl.

Nothing could've been further from the truth, but it resulted in a battle far too many girls end up in. Natalie was a casualty of anorexia and bulimia.

About the time I came back from my second stint at Ozanam, Natalie was just coming back from an eating disorder clinic in San Diego. Her school locker was a few over from mine, and being kind of kindred new kids to the school, we connected.

As the year went on, I noticed a pattern. Natalie would randomly disappear for weeks at a time and then show up again. I didn't have to ask to know what that meant.

We'd often sit together at lunch. She was the most giving person I had ever met, and she would often try to force her food onto my tray. But I never accepted. One day she turned to me and said, "Levi, your friendship has literally saved my life. I hope someday I can return the favor."

And in time she would get the chance to do just that.

During my couchsurfing period in the summer, Natalie was one person who made it her mission to see that I was okay. I know she tried to get her folks to help, but her family lived in a multimillion-dollar house and, while I was allowed to visit, I would sometimes catch her mom using Lysol on any chair I had sat in.

Natalie helped me keep my mind off my current crisis and back on the moment. One summer day I was at her house killing some time before I went to the next house to crash, when she goaded me into going for a walk. It was pretty hot, but her neighborhood was beautiful with huge trees and manicured yards.

"Levi, there is someone I want you to meet." We were walking down the street of ritzy mansions toward the pool. "Would you please come to church with me tonight, just once?" A sweet smile graced Natalie's thin face.

"Sure, why not?" I nodded, and we continued our walk and conversation.

I did it for her, but I didn't know what I was getting myself into.

The air of the basement room was chilly, just shy of a shiver. Natalie and I were a bit late to her youth group, and the kids were already singing a song I remembered as a kid.

We took our seats. I could instantly see something different in Natalie. She seemed more free and at ease than she did at our school filled with shallow teenagers, or in her home with rigid and somewhat snobbish parents.

Then I saw why.

A college-age girl came up behind Natalie and threw her arms around her. Natalie spun in response, and the two squealed in delight to see each other. I rolled my eyes. *Girls.*

But at the same time, I nearly had to force my mouth closed.

Natalie's friend was hands down the most beautiful person I'd ever met. She would stand out in any crowd with her radiant smile, deep olive skin, and long, smooth black hair. Even her words sounded beautiful, pronounced with a deep Latin accent.

The two of them spoke for a couple minutes while the kids around us just kept doing their thing: hands raised, tears streaming, random jumping. Before long, the girl broke away, went up front, and grabbed the microphone.

"Levi," Natalie whispered in my ear and pointed, "that's Naomi. She's from Brazil."

I nodded my head. I wanted to move to Brazil. Like right now!

All the kids returned to their seats as Naomi began talking to the group. "She's who I wanted you to meet."

After youth group, Natalie and I hung out while Naomi made her way around the room, talking and hugging the various kids. Then came our turn. Naomi hugged Natalie again, but then Natalie pulled a fast one and said she had to get home, leaving Naomi and me alone.

"You hungry, Levi?" Naomi asked, walking around, turning off the lights to the youth room. "We can hit Mickey D's on our way out if you like. My treat?"

I smiled. "Yeah, I could eat." Like always!

We made our way into the golden arches, placed our order, and sat down in a booth in the back corner. Naomi ripped open a tub of barbeque sauce and went right into both the food and the conversation.

"You'll have to forgive her, but Natalie told me most of what has been going on with you." She dipped a handful of fries into the sauce. "That girl, let me tell you, can be quite the talker sometimes—but she means well." She winked and flashed a bright white smile.

"It's cool. I trust her." I wasn't really sure what to say. Seems Naomi knew where she was going with this, and I did not. But I could listen to Naomi's accent all night, so I wasn't in a hurry to go anywhere.

"Well, I have to say, what you're going through is not cool, really not cool, and I want to help. I've been there myself, and I know what it's like not being able to trust people. So before I dare to ask you to trust me, I want to share with you who I am and where I have come from, if that's cool with you?" Naomi had a peaceful way with every word she said, and I found myself relaxing in her presence.

I leaned over and bit into my burger. "Sure, I got time." For the next hour I sat and listened as she poured out her heart, her life, and what she'd made of it.

Naomi was somewhat of an orphan herself, having been abandoned by her family a few years back. She'd grown up in Brazil in an emotionally cold house, where she was sexually abused for many of her young years and beaten if she resisted or did not *please*. One day she couldn't take it anymore and ran away. For two years she drifted, sleeping in abandoned cars and dark alleys. There were times she found herself losing the survival battle, so she'd get drunk and end up letting some man use her in trade for a place to stay for the night. Even if it was a stranger's arms in a motel room, sometimes that was better than one more night alone on the streets.

But a day came when a rescue line was dropped into the pit of her life. She met an American missionary in the slums of Rio de Janeiro. Through him she learned of something called *hope* and realized she needed a change. Over the next weeks, Naomi came to peace with God, and before the young missionary left, she asked if she could follow him to the states. He gladly said yes.

A couple years later, a citizenship, and now working her way through college, here we were, sitting in a fast-food restaurant eating hamburgers and fries while I listened to her story.

I couldn't help but see the power of what she was sharing from her own life. She told me how her life would be over—dead in some alley or garbage heap in Rio—if it hadn't been for God's endless love that changed her. She'd been able to let all the hurt go and follow after God.

No wonder the kids packed that basement youth room. If her story wasn't enough to move you, her very presence would. Naomi was a vibrant flower in a world full of weeds. Every facet of her, who she was as a person, begged you to trust her.

"Levi, now that you have heard where I came from, what I've been through"—Naomi jabbed the straw down through a chunk of ice for the last sip of her soda—"what do you think?"

"You're definitely a mess," I chuckled. "Just like me."

"You are right-on with that." We both smiled. "Levi, do you think God cares about *your* mess?"

I exhaled and paused. How did I know it was going to come to this?

"No." Even to my own ears I sounded indignant. But that was too bad. She was the one who brought up the subject. "I honestly don't. Besides, why would he?"

"'Cause maybe he loves you!" Her voice was warmer than before. "Levi, you don't know that he loves you, do you?"

"Not really. I've seen the opposite."

"Why is that?" I could tell by her demeanor that she seemed heartbroken by my statement.

"Naomi, I'm sorry, and not trying to be ungrateful and all, but was talking about this part of the meal deal?"

"No, it wasn't. I'm sorry." She paused for a moment. "It's just hard for me to see someone going through the same pain I've been through and not know their heart and them mine. Can I ask why you don't feel he loves you? Is it just because of you, or do you feel he doesn't care about us, period?"

I had never thought about it that way before. Did God love and help some people—beautiful people like Naomi—and leave others, like me, to wallow in misery?

"I guess it's a mix of both. Why?"

"Levi, he *does* love you, and he loves all of us. It's us … our hearts … that keep us from seeing, from believing that." Naomi continued to look at me. "You do believe he exists, right?"

"Of course." I paused and sucked up some soda. "I mean, look around us. This world, all the animals, nature, didn't just happen from a cosmic fart. But that doesn't mean he loves me."

"Levi, if you believe he is there when you can't see him, then why don't you believe he loves? Because you can't see it, or should I say feel it?"

Naomi had me there. But I wasn't willing to blindly follow like the other basement kids.

"For one, look at my life … look at *your* life." I paused, having realized what I just said. "Okay, I take it back about you, but really look at my life. How can you say *this* is love? Naomi, say you loved me. Would you let any of this happen? My mom … Allen … being a homeless kid? Would you? Of course you wouldn't, 'cause no one lets someone they love hang out to dry!"

Naomi's eyes filled with tears, and I wondered if I had been too hard in what I'd said. And there was an awkward silence.

"Levi, allowing something to happen doesn't mean he doesn't love you or any of us. It just means—" Naomi paused, dabbing at her eyes with a napkin. "It just means that he is there, even in the silence."

I was trying to hold back a laugh. That made no sense. "I'm sorry, Naomi. Was there more to where you were going with that?"

Naomi sniffled as she leaned across the table. "Levi, that's just it, there's always more with him. We can't define God with our simplistic languages or humanistic viewpoints … with words … with ideas. God isn't that simple. It would be like me trying to define you with a few simple words. How would that feel?"

"Well, if you did, I'd probably tell you to go take a flying leap off a bridge." I shot her a smile, letting her know I was only half-serious. I remembered some of the words Allen had used on me, simple words, words meant to define me as someone I wasn't. "But it's happened to me before, and it really stunk."

"Sometimes he is silent, and sometimes he isn't, Levi, and this side of heaven we will never know why, no matter how hard it hurts. But what if despite the silence and the pain, we can get past ourselves, our close-minded preconceived notions, and just let ourselves experience God … while *in* these moments of pain?" Naomi reached out and put her hand on top of mine. "Don't you think if we could experience God in those moments, we could really begin to get what he is all about, who he is? Maybe that is why the silence is there—to help us find him in it?"

What she was saying made sense, and I gave a grudging nod. "A wise man I knew not too long ago said something along those lines."

"Yeah?" She began to smile, seeing that something was registering with me. "What did he say?"

"I dunno, exactly … it was really deep. Something like life being a hurricane that you can't get out of … and that you should go to the middle of it, to the eye, where God is … so you can have peace." I was trying my best to repeat what Chaplain Wes had said. "That only in the middle of life's storms can we find God's peace in *spite* of the chaos."

A huge grin spread across her face. "Wow, that's really good. You care if I use that at youth group?"

"By all means. Besides, it's obviously not my wisdom or we wouldn't be having this talk." We both laughed.

It was getting late, and one of the kids behind the register walked to our table. Closing time. Naomi and I hadn't paid any attention to the hour.

"Levi, before we go, I have to ask you something." Naomi had a more serious look again. "Can you let go of all your pain? Will you let God have it?"

What does she mean let him have it? Isn't it kind of his fault I'm drowning in it in the first place? Besides, what would that look like to let God have my pain?

"Levi, will you let God come into your life—into your heart—and live?"

We had come full circle. My personal history and pain was the whole reason we were here. Seems I had amassed a lot of that history in my seventeen years, and Naomi had experienced awful things too. I could trust her.

But could I trust him? That remained to be seen.

Besides, I was used to the pain. If not exactly safe, it was comfortable and familiar. To let that go was uncharted territory, almost like becoming someone else—a new person. That was scary. Change had never been a good thing in my life. Better to leave things as they were.

Anyhow, this love she kept speaking of—his love—I was more scared of that. How could I know that he could love me? Truth was, he was probably like everyone else I had let in. He'd get to know me, take one look around, and leave like all the rest.

Naomi knew my struggle firsthand, and I wanted so badly to have what she had. Hope. And love. But another four-letter word held me back.

Fear.

"I'm sorry, Naomi." I looked into her eyes. "I don't think I can."

Naomi nodded her head, and a tear shook loose and landed on the table. "I understand, Levi. I really do."

We sat there in silence for a few moments before once again being reminded that the lobby was closing. My mind drifted to what I thought love was, why I was given up on by so many, passed by, and why I was seemingly unlovable.

Was love even real, or was it a mirage, something hoped for in the distance as I wandered through this hardened world? Naomi was probably remembering her own heartache as we sat together.

Once again love slipped away.

Yet this time, I was the one pushing it.

16

LOVE STANDS AT THE DOOR

The door's unlocked, come on in! Make yourself at home, God. What's mine is yours!"

That should have been my answer that day in response to Naomi's question. Back then, things with me were never that simple—they still probably aren't. My heart was a locked-down fortress—hardened, impenetrable. No one could get in and I didn't *want* anyone in—not even God himself.

I trusted no one.

And the result? I was alone. All *alone*.

⌁

My thoughts flashed back to when I was a kid: "Mommy, why is God standing at the door? How can he open it when there isn't a doorknob?"

"Because you can only let him in from the inside."

I was the only one who could let God in, and once again I left love standing out in the cold. But why hold out and push away the one thing I longed for?

Fear.

Specifically, I feared that God was like people. That he would come into my life, take one look around, and walk away like so many others had. Some left without saying good-bye, some left because their days on this earth had come to an end, and others left because I was not what they wanted. Still, they all left. And I was alone.

A kid left alone in *this* world? Those aren't very good odds. But I had my doubts that anyone could ever really be trusted to stay with me, let alone love me.

I never found out how Naomi felt that night when I said no. And knowing what I know now, having walked the same road, almost, I know it had to tear her up inside.

Naomi, the woman of deep strength that she was, spun the conversation in another direction as we walked out to her car. She rummaged through her purse for her keys.

"Well, dude, I have a place for you to stay for a while." Her smile radiated underneath the parking lot light. "My boyfriend lives with some other college guys across town, and would love to take you in … that is if you're cool staying with a bunch of smelly, overgrown boys."

I laughed. "They ain't got nothing on me. I haven't showered in days!"

She laughed with me and took a step back as she playfully held her hand up over her nose. "Yeah, I got a whiff of that at the table. It's all good, though—I've been there myself. Nevertheless, I still love you, kid."

Like many times before, I was riding in a car to go stay with someone I had never met. But unlike the days in foster care, this was different. I wasn't apprehensive.

Naomi's boyfriend, Parker, was in his midtwenties and in a summer internship program working as a church youth pastor. He was a cool guy: lean, smart, and had a nearly shaved buzz cut that hinted black, if he'd ever let it grow out. He went to school in the heart of the state at the University of Missouri, where he played lacrosse. Truth be told, Parker could have gone to any Ivy League college to play lacrosse, and a few had asked him—he was that good. But he turned them all down to stay close to home, close to Naomi, and close to the church he was involved with.

Parker was a quiet sort, but far from stoic—he was just a man of few words. And when he did speak, everything he said had a kind of charismatic wisdom about it. He was just the guy to take in a punk kid like me.

We arrived at the house close to midnight, and Parker was out on the front steps waiting for us. When our car stopped, he opened the passenger side door where I sat.

I stuck my hand out in introduction. "Hey, man, how are you?"

"Good, brother. You ready to do this?" He flashed a charming smile and grabbed my hand, pulling me toward him in one of those ritualistic man-hugs called "dap."

So began my days with Parker and the college guys. The house the lot of them lived in was initially meant for college guys, but Parker pulled a few strings and got it cleared for a "teen runaway" to take refuge there with them, and they took me in as one of their own.

For the rest of the summer, I shadowed Parker everywhere he went, which at times was hard to do since he was a man always on the go. Parker looked out for me and treated me like family; so did the other guys he lived with: Mac, Paul, and Joey. The way they lived, their lives, spoke to something I had never seen before. Was this what love looked like? Whatever it was, it wasn't a gang, and it sure wasn't what I had known of foster care.

⁓

When summer drew to a close, the guys had to take off to their respective colleges, which left me looking for a place to land, too. My senior year of high school loomed close, and I was thankful when my buddy Matt came through with a place for me to stay. One of his friend's parents was getting divorced and needed someone to stay in their home while they parted ways and let the courts settle who got what. All they asked was that I not tear up their house, be respectful, and treat their belongings as if my own.

I thought I could handle that.

The Smiths' house had a large spread of land that backed up to the Missouri River Valley. I was asked to take care of the land, keep the acreage mowed, and put everything away for winter if neither one of them had returned by then. In addition to a roof over my head, they paid the utilities, paid me to stay there, and gave me an additional food allowance. Ms. Boyden was even able to get a school bus to divert its route by two miles and pick me up.

I moved in two days before my senior year started. The Smiths were long gone. Mrs. Smith had moved herself and the kids in with her parents in northern Iowa, and Mr. Smith worked for the government out in Virginia during the week, and he decided to stay out there until things got sorted back home. This left me with free reign of the house—sort of.

I basically lost touch with Parker and the other guys I'd grown close to when they went back to school. Naomi also went on a semester-long mission trip to Puerto Rico. Once again, I was back to going it alone.

And I won't lie, it hurt—even though I know that was the farthest thing from their intentions.

They had become what I had longed for: family.

Matt was able to help me get my job back at the Apple Market, and we started hanging out a lot again. Maybe too much. He was a partier, and I began to drift. When we weren't at work or school, he would come to the Smiths,' and we'd smoke a blunt or two or drink a few beers, most times both. I learned quickly the easiest way to get rid of pain, the laziest way, was to get messed up. Besides, you'll forget the bad times if you kill off the brain cells that hold those memories. It didn't take long for me to go hard after the high or buzz the drugs offered, even if they were the "socially acceptable" ones.

I had one goal: to shut up the voice screaming from inside that I hurt, that I was lonely. *Anything* to stop its relentless nagging, because it reminded me of how powerless I was to stop the pain.

Even as I set foot on the road to destroying myself, I never once missed school. Kind of an oxymoron. Yes, I hated my past as much as it hated me, but I didn't want to mess with my future, even when I believed the lies that I wouldn't have one.

Then came a day that changed everything in the life of everyone around me.

17

BLOOD, SWEAT, AND TEARS

It was a picture-perfect day, sunny and mild for early September. But the peaceful morning was interrupted when a handful of deluded men thought it wise to fly jetliners into the heart of American symbolism—our economic structure, our military prowess.

Loved ones were lost, and we could no longer ignore one word—terrorism—as if it didn't exist and return to the life we had known before.

In those foolish acts that late summer morning, they reawakened a slumbering giant and rightfully earned what would soon come their way. A fireball of hatred changed our lives and would soon end theirs.

This was war, and now she was on our soil.

I was a senior in high school, sitting in my first-period language arts class with Ms. Colburn. Resting my head on my desk helped my hangover a little, and I draped an arm over my face to block out the light. Occasionally I'd prop myself up to down another swig of Gatorade. A throbbing headache reverberated around my cranium, a reminder that I'd spent the night before in the unforgiving company of Jack Daniels.

Our classroom door came open with a sudden *swoosh*, and the teacher from next door, Mrs. Johnston, rushed in.

"You have to see this!" Mrs. Johnston said to Ms. Colburn, and strode to the classroom television to turn it on.

The images became increasingly clear on the old analog TV as the tube came to life with a radiant buzz. Centered on the screen was one of the World Trade Center towers. A gaping hole spewed an inferno of flames that lapped up the side and billowed smoke for miles around.

"Some kind of passenger jet flew into it a few minutes ago," Mrs. Johnston said.

"Was it an accident?" Ms. Colburn, alarmed, walked slowly forward, her gaze never leaving the screen.

"No one knows, but what is a 737 doing flying that low near Manhattan?"

Every one of us in the classroom sat with eyes glued to the drama unfolding, as we listened to the reporters' every word to learn what had happened.

A small eternity later, while the camera feed from a news chopper focused on the flames, a small image appeared on the outer frame of the screen. Before my brain could connect that it too was a passenger jet, the ghostly figure flew full speed into the second tower and buried itself deep inside. A gigantic fireball filled with glass and metal erupted out the other side and rained shrapnel onto the streets below.

"*Whoaaaa!*" a collective gasp chorused through the classroom.

No one had to say anything. This wasn't an accident—not twice in the same place.

The end-of-period bell interrupted our absorption with the drama. I assumed the entire school knew by now, as very few students socialized in the hallway during the break. Like me, most rushed to our lockers, grabbed what we needed, and then darted to our next class.

That class happened to be with Mrs. Johnston for current events, and there was nothing more current in the world than the terror unfolding on her television.

I went right to my seat but had barely gotten settled when the newsman broke into the visual feed and switched to another camera in a different location. We were now staring at a building I had seen a few times before in history class. It too lay in flames. "This just in. The Pentagon has been struck by a third aircraft."

The Pentagon was hit?

No one spoke as we watched our country come under attack. But why? This couldn't be another country attacking us. If it was, they wouldn't go after civilians, nor would they hit us at the brain trust of our military. They would hit us muscle for muscle, military to military, like wars are supposed to be fought. We all sensed this was different, and we couldn't help being terrified.

The man on the television announced there was reason to believe there was a fourth plane heading toward Washington, targeting either the Capitol or White House, and that the president and his staff were being moved to an undisclosed bunker.

Regardless of political party, the White House is *our* house, and the president is our man. You don't go there. You don't go after him.

Mrs. Johnston cycled between the news stations, but the coverage was all the same. One station had a camera zoomed into the towers, where people could be seen hanging out of broken windows. Desperate for air, some hung their upper bodies out to escape the choking smoke and flame inside.

And then it happened.

We all watched in horror as the camera showed people plummeting from the towers, human beings forced by the inferno into the most terrible of decisions. I gripped the edge of my desk and held back tears. Anger lumped in my throat. Those were people, with names, families, loved ones, whose lives were now over because of the hideous actions of a few. I turned to the girl beside me and, with the tears now released and sliding down my face, I nudged her on the arm.

"When we find out who did this, we better hit them back—and hard!"

When we thought the day couldn't get any worse, we watched live and in color as the first tower looked as if it was swaying in the wind. Then it buckled and gave way, crashing to the earth and spreading a cloud of toxic ash for what looked like miles around.

"Oh, my God. Oh … my …" Mrs. Johnston gripped the edge of her desk and vomited into the trash can. We wept as one, knowing that countless people had just died in the worst national catastrophe any of us had seen in our lifetime.

The day crawled by, a slow-motion slideshow of crashing planes, tumbling skyscrapers, and burning buildings. Sometimes I wanted to pinch myself to see if this was all real. By the time the sun set, the

Pentagon lay crumbled with a burnt scar on her face, the fourth plane was in a debris-strewn trench in a Pennsylvania field, our president was hidden away for safe keeping, and both towers, along with everyone inside, were gone.

While we may have gotten punched in the mouth that day, the thing about America is that however imperfect we may be or politically divided we are at times, when we're tested we come *together*. And we won't stay down, not for long. *We the people* will get back up, and when we do, you have a world of hurt coming.

Seizing upon our American spirit, recruiters from all branches of the military came to school the next day during the lunch hour. I had gotten my tray of food and was weaving through chairs toward a table when I spotted them over against the far wall. A few kids were already talking with the uniformed recruiters. I wolfed down my food and headed their direction. I already knew which branch I was going to talk to; I had known for years. But yesterday's attack cemented my decision.

"Son, what's your name?" Sergeant Wolcowitz asked, sticking his hand out. "And are there any questions you might have I can answer?"

"It's Levi, and no … I'm good. I want to join up."

I'm not sure why he was taken aback. Maybe my bluntness, or that I still had food in the corners of my mouth. He stood with a puzzled look for a moment, then gave a little chuckle before continuing in his deep Southern drawl.

"So you want to enlist." He looked me up and down. "What is it you want to do for the army?"

"When we go to war, I want to be in on hunting the people down who did this. And when the time comes, you know … kill 'em."

There was a silence as we stared at each other. Neither of us flinched.

"Well, kid, that'd be an Eleven Bravo—that's the infantry. And trust me, I get where you're coming from. I think we all feel that way, and we'll get them sooner or later—we will!"

On September 25, 2001, I was officially sworn in to the US Army. After signing my name a few hundred times to complete the transaction, I was now the property of the government.

I was scheduled to ship out for Basic Training the upcoming May, so to bide my time I chose to take part in the Delayed Entry Program, in which you train in the basic army fundamentals before you go active. The reward is a rank advancement.

As on the day I first met Sergeant Wolcowitz, I wanted to get in on hunting down the fools that did this, so I chose to be an Eleven Bravo, the military occupational code assigned to an infantryman.

There was a small hiccup to going off to war just then: I still had to graduate high school. Before I could be handed a rifle, I needed to be handed a diploma. So it was back to being a kid again.

The remainder of my senior year went by in slow motion, and my classes and homework assignments seemed irrelevant to my future as a soldier. Since I had been a young boy sitting on my father's shoulders at the Blue Angels airshow, I wanted to be in the military. Now that dream was real and close, and it helped me focus on the future and bury the nightmare of my past.

I was still working part time, going to school full time, and trying to keep out of trouble. But trouble and me had a chronic dysfunctional relationship. Matt, though a good friend, was no help at all in that regard. One day he brought his dealer over to smoke with us at the Smith house.

In his midtwenties, Phillip was a hardened thug to the core, the kind whose fate lay behind bars or in the grave. Both his older brothers were serving consecutive life sentences for a gas-station robbery that had left two people dead. He'd been raised in the same posh neighborhood Natalie's family called home. But he loathed the lifestyle of the rich and famous—which also required hard work—and wanted respect earned the dirty way. He had dropped out of school and gone to live with his dealer to become a disciple of sorts in the ways of hustling. He reminded me of my cousin Wyatt.

It wasn't long before I started hanging out with him regularly. Phillip would often pick me up from school or the Smiths' house to go on drug runs. I was just knuckle dragging with him, killing time.

I even got homemade tattoos courtesy of his girlfriend. Phillip's was some oriental dragon rolling up his back. I chose to get a skull with two rifles crossed behind it inked onto my shoulder. It had a banner scrolling around it that read, *Mess wit' the best-Die like the rest-U.S. Army.* The idea came from an old patch I had seen at the VFW with my grandpa.

I continued being a shortsighted moron. And right before my eighteenth birthday, Phillip came to me with a business proposition of sorts. His supplier was getting paranoid that the Feds were watching him, and he was clearing out mass amounts of drugs for cheap.

"You got two hundred fifty dollars to throw in on this?" Phillip asked, finishing the last hit off our Swisher Sweet filled with pot.

I leaned for my wallet and tossed him what cash I had. A few hours later, Phillip came through on his word—and then some. When he walked in the door, he pulled a massive, heavily wrinkled brown paper sack out of his coat. Inside was a Ziploc filled with two pounds of black tar opium.

"You got that from him?" My eyes lit up in shock. "For two fifty!"

"Yeah, cuz," Phillip slurred. Most likely he had tried some on his way over. "For real, don't get caught slinging this, cause it's straight-up heroin. This right here … it'll get you life and then some."

Phillip leaned over—just shy of falling on his face—and handed me the cannonball-sized wad of narcotics. "If you nickel and dime it, you can dig about four, say five k's of green in yo' pockets."

I slid a glance at him while calculating the math to see if he was right. "You for real about this?"

"Yup. It's legit, man." Phillip collapsed into the recliner and nodded off.

The math was right on, too, and that was the end of my money problems. After playing wanna-be drug dealer for a little over a week, I had sold every last gram—except what Phillip and I had smoked— and pocketed more than $4,300. I hired the lawyer I had needed for the past year, got a car, and was on my way.

Before I could become Phillip the second, the cavalry rode to my rescue—the cavalry being the US Army. During the process of my enlistment, Sergeant Wolcowitz had misplaced a few pieces of paperwork relating to my days at Ozanam, so we needed to go back to the enlistment station and do them over. When we got there, wouldn't you know they pulled a random drug test per Sergeant Wolcowitz's request.

A week later, he pulled me aside.

"Levi, get over here." Sergeant Wolcowitz was staring at something he had just pulled from the fax machine, and I could tell by his voice that he knew. "You failed your drop with flying colors."

I sat in the chair by his desk without a word.

"Just what do you think you're doing?" The chew under his lip began to poke out under the velocity of his words. "You wanna be a pothead or a soldier?"

Busted!

I wasn't dumb, and there was no need to lie—not to him. So I kept my trap shut.

"Let me tell you something, Shepherd—I get it. I get what you are trying to run from. I have read every page of your file front to back a dozen times." He quieted a little. "I know the voices you are trying to silence, but son, believe me, this isn't the way."

He reached in his lip, pulled out his dip, and flung it into the trash beneath his desk. "Now, let me tell you something else, Levi. You know the strings I have pulled to erase your record? You even know why I went to such efforts? Because I believe in you, even if you don't and there sure seem to be few that have. So show me some respect, and knock this off! You got me?"

I looked at him and nodded, mystified by held-back tears. I wasn't choked up because I was being yelled at, but because he was right.

"One last thing. You got what it takes, kid. Now, take that pain and those voices and let it fuel you to become the most fearsome warrior you can be. And I promise you that will make all that pain worthwhile!"

We sat there for a few seconds as he waited to see if I was going to back down from his challenge to give it my all or go home. Thing was, I didn't have a home to go to. The army was it. If I wanted it, I had to fight for it, starting today.

"What do you think?"

"I think you're right, Sergeant." I wiped the last tear from my eye. "I just don't know how to get there, you know? I still got today to worry about, and man, today sucks!"

"*You* might believe that, but *I* don't. You know what I see when I see you? I see someone orphaned by his own blood, someone with a history of gangs, violence, and shoot, let's not forget foster care. Yet, Levi, that's not who you are. Because when I look at you, I see all that, but I see it making you—*if you let it*—into a man whom many will follow."

I was covered with goose bumps from his love and encouragement.

"Let me ask you this: Are you going to do this for real, or are you going to be like everyone else when backed against a wall?"

"No, Sergeant, I'm in!"

"All right. That's what I thought!" Sergeant Wolcowitz stood from behind his desk and walked toward the back door of the office. "Your training starts now. Get out and run thirty laps around the parking lot before we call it a night."

It didn't sound too bad, but it was a huge parking lot. Those thirty laps were more like five miles.

18

OPTION 40

Sergeant Wolcowitz took me under his wing and began to grind off those jagged edges where I needed to be broken down. Every day after school he collected me—no more hanging with Matt or Phillip—and he'd send me out to the strip mall parking lot to run laps … *countless* laps. When I was done running, he kept me busting out push-ups and sit-ups.

At first I couldn't do it, at least not in the time restraints he gave me. But I soon started hitting his marks, and then he'd make it harder. Despite being far from out of shape when we first began, even for a pothead, I was soon in the best shape of my life—*fighting* shape.

And Sergeant Wolcowitz took notice of my efforts.

The sergeant was career army, and this was his first gig as a recruiter. The office lifestyle was not really his thing, just something to notch off in hopes of getting into OCS (Officer Candidate School) so he could rise the ranks in the army and one day retire as a distinguished officer.

He was ten years in and had already traveled more places and seen and done things others had not. And Sergeant Wolcowitz was gung ho, same as me. He had served in a military intelligence unit during the Bosnian conflict while attached to a 10th Special Forces A-Team.

Sergeant Wolcowitz was a man who could distinguish the men from the boys and those who could wage war from those who just played it. That came from serving with some of the most elite our country has to offer, and from his brief days as a drill sergeant— brief because he was pulled from that post for reasons I don't fully know, though he once hinted that he had mouthed off to someone he shouldn't have and it had cost him dearly.

If anyone was going to make a man of me, take a punk kid and turn him into a solider, the sergeant was. And he did it with delight.

In our early days together, he asked me what I wanted to be. My answer: *the best.* I had voices deep in my heart—from my past, from my present—that screamed at me that I was nobody, an alone nobody. I had to shut them up, either by drugging them or by proving them wrong.

I wanted to get in the war and do what I could. Maybe one day I'd become a general and serve with distinction, and when my time was done, ride off into the sunset, and work for the CIA. But I had to prove myself first. To myself more than others.

Sergeant Wolcowitz wasn't going to cut me any slack, either. I had scored a ninety-two on my ASVAB, which is the military aptitude test, similar to the SAT. Ninety-nine was a perfect score, so I was up there. I had also scored perfect in the combat arms section, and that got his attention all the more.

Between my drive, test scores, and what Sergeant Wolcowitz saw in me, he decided to make it his personal mission to make me *all that I could be,* and he knew just which direction to send me in the army— the Army Rangers.

He rode my hide mercilessly, never letting me forget I could be a commando, until that was the only identity I could see for myself. At the parking lot of the recruiter's station, along with several weekends out at Fort Leavenworth not far outside of Kansas City, I trained for him—and then trained some more. I learned that pain, though ever so real, was a lie. Pain isn't *who* you are and, no matter how strong, it can never take away *who* you are unless you let it.

Three months into my tutelage with this recruiter-gone-crazy, he pulled me aside at the office one night as he was getting ready to take me home.

"Listen, Levi." He laid his hand on my shoulder and looked me in the eye. "I've pulled a few favors and arranged something for you tomorrow that I need you to give everything you got. This could change your future and could get you a spot held in Ranger Qualification. You think you can handle that?"

"Yes." I nodded my head and shook his hand in thanks. "I will, Sergeant."

Snow whipped through the air in a fierce blizzard the next day as Sergeant Wolcowitz and I drove the government-plated Ford sedan along the highway, making our way through the Missouri River Valley and over to Fort Leavenworth. We were scheduled to meet an old colleague of the sergeant, a man named Captain Bowers, whom he had served with in Bosnia. The captain was at Leavenworth for a few weeks taking part in a training exercise at the SAMS (School of Advanced Military Studies) located at the base.

Our drive took an eternity—well, that's how it seemed to me, anyway—on a miserable day when most normal people would have stayed indoors. But not us; not for this. After all, if you're going to be a commando, you train and fight regardless of the conditions around you.

When we arrived, I saw the ghostly image of a man through the foggy, iced windshield. He was wrapped in a long, military trench coat, his back to the wind as he dodged the frigid blasts of air whipping across the running trail. He stood there as if frozen or uncaring that we had just pulled up.

We got out of the car and walked into the howling wind toward the shadowy figure.

"This the punk kid you were telling me about?" The man's voice sliced through the flying snow as we reached him.

"Yes, sir, it is." Sergeant Wolcowitz looked at me. "Captain Bowers, I would like to introduce you to Private Shepherd."

We both saluted the captain. He returned it, and we were set at ease.

"Sergeant Wolcowitz seems to have great faith in you, son." Captain Bowers looked the part of a Special Forces commando: fit physique, steely, merciless eyes. He stood in his dress uniform: a braided blue Infantry Cord adorned his shoulder, several medals crested his chest, and atop his head lay the iconic and feared beret.

"He says you got what it takes to be a Ranger. Truth be told, kid, I don't care who you are, but I trust this man with my life. He saved my hide back in the day, and if he says something, I'm inclined to listen." He shot a glance at Sergeant Wolcowitz, then returned his stare to me. "Long and short, kid, you best not be wasting my time!"

"Sir, he's ready," the sergeant said.

"He better be." Captain Bowers faced me and pointed to his headwear. "Private, do you know what this is?"

"Sir, I do—it's the Green Beret."

"That's right. And do you know how I got this? I got it by putting in my time and paying my dues to a life that requires the utmost of sacrifices. It also means I play by my own rules." He took a step back and pointed to the track behind him. "Each lap is exactly one mile long. The sergeant here brags you can run a flat six. Well, today you have to run two miles in eleven minutes. You got one shot, kid. There are no second chances. Understood?"

"Yes, sir, I do."

"That's good, because your time started one minute ago!"

For a split second I thought I had heard him wrong. Then my brain put his words together with his stern countenance. Captain Bowers was serious.

I took off running as fast as I could. We had come here today so that I could perform in front of Captain Bowers the same PT requirements an Army Ranger has to perform. And here I was, tearing down the track in a blizzard, fighting the side gusts that shoved me off course, and I had to do it in under the time I had trained for. And that was to be expected. After all, you seldom, if ever, got to choose the places or conditions in which you fought, and you still had to complete the objective.

But a five-minute mile—not even Jesse Owens could do that in *this* weather.

I don't know what possessed me to even try. Maybe it was the voices that antagonized me from the past. I didn't care that I was probably going to fail. I ran. Deep inside, I wanted this—to be the best. To squelch the pain, erase the past, and to put an end to those who had started this war.

Halfway through the first lap, I hit a patch of ice underneath the layer of snow and wiped out headfirst, as if I were sliding into home plate. I stood back up. I had scraped my elbow and gashed a hole in my windbreakers on jagged ice, revealing a bleeding and throbbing knee. I ignored the wounds, shook off the pain, and took off again. Each step sent fire radiating from my busted knee.

Sweaty, wet, and bloody, I pounded down the track with everything I had. I knew I wasn't going to make the mark, but I wasn't going to give up. This track became the symbol of my life: a setup to fail.

I refused to give up.

I had come too far, been through too much to give up now.

I finished the first lap, passing the two men watching me as they stood as silhouettes against the swirling white.

"Seven minutes, seventeen seconds, Shepherd," Captain Bowers yelled through the flurry. "You sure you got this in you? Think about it: you got to run the rest in under four. Even on a good day, you can't do that. Why don't you give up and come get warm?"

"Ignore that, Levi!" Sergeant Wolcowitz's voice drowned out the captain. "Just run and run some more. You got this, kid. You can do this!"

Maybe I was delusional, but I ran harder than I ever had in all my life. Every lungful of air stitched needles in my sides. Snot and tears covered my face, nearly frozen in place from the wind.

Coming into the last corner, I pushed all the harder, and when I saw where the finish was, I flew down the track, heart in my throat and my vision going red from lack of oxygen to my brain.

"Done!" Sergeant Wolcowitz shouted as I crossed the line.

I had barely registered those words when my legs gave out and I collapsed in a heap on the side of the track. I tried to get back on my feet as I choked on the very air my body craved and hot saliva ran from my mouth.

"Walk it off, Levi, walk it off," Captain Bowers said, as the two of them came toward me. "Your body needs air. Get up and walk, son."

I stumbled around, and my legs buckled again. Bile shot into my mouth, and I leaned over as it fell out onto the snow, choosing that over forcing it back down. As the captain had ordered, I struggled to regain my footing on the slippery track.

"Sir," I panted, "what's my time?" I wiped the gruel from my mouth with my sleeve.

"Doesn't matter, Shepherd," Captain Bowers said, offering a hand up. He shot a look to Sergeant Wolcowitz, but my brain couldn't process the nonverbal communication between the two men.

"Sir, please, what's my—"

"Private, I don't care about your time. It never mattered. I asked you to do something you knew you had no chance of doing, yet you still gave it your all. That's what I came to see today—heart—whether you had it or not, because that's what separates the best from the rest. Those who'll fight on even when they know they will lose. Those who will fight to their dying breath. Heart, son ... it's *all* about heart." Captain Bowers looked me in the eye, removed his glove, and offered me his warm hand. "And, kid, you have it in spades."

We all walked to the car. "Private, I'll sign off for you to go Option 40. Now, go prove yourself to be part of the best." He turned to Sergeant Wolcowitz. "Oh, and Scott ... drinks are on you this weekend."

"Roger that, sir." Sergeant Wolcowitz saluted, then the captain headed toward a distant building. The sergeant turned to me with a smile that said it all.

Kid, you got what it takes. Now go be the best.

⁓⌁⁓

Sergeant Wolcowitz's faith in me was not in vain. When he was done with me, I was Private First Class, having advanced in rank twice before going active duty.

Seems I had finally found my calling in life.

19

THE PLACES YOU'LL GO

When you have a dream, it renews hope, strengthens your heart, and gives you the stamina to endure the challenges ahead, no matter how difficult.

In seventeen years, I'd had a lot of brutal challenges *without* that dream. But now it was my chance to live out my future. Of course, first I had to graduate high school.

———

A couple of weeks into the new semester after the Christmas break, Ms. Boyden invited me into her office.

"Kiddo, I have some bad news." I could tell by the look on her face that whatever it was hurt her, too. "I don't know how we didn't catch this until now, but your credits from Ozanam aren't matching up in some classes, and well ..."—she paused, as if to hold back tears— "you're a half-credit short. You aren't going to be graduating on time. You need to let Sergeant Wolcowitz know."

I couldn't go active into the army or Ranger school without graduating.

"I know you need this, so worst case I can help you get your GED." She stood and, with tears in her eyes, pulled me into her arms for a hug. "Whatever we have to do to get you to Fort Benning, I promise I am with you every step of the way."

But I wasn't going to settle for a GED. I could have gone that route months ago when all this began. Sure, I was messed up in a lot of ways, but one thing I'd done against all odds was to stay in school.

No, going the GED path wasn't an option for me.

Disheartened by the news, I headed home to the Smiths' house. As I slumped on the couch wondering what to do, the phone rang.

I'd lost touch with Parker after summer when he and the other guys had gone back to college, but he looked me up when he came back for Christmas. With endless apologies for "bailing" on me, he had vowed to stay in touch and call me once a week. Now, when I answered the phone, Parker was on the other end.

"Hey, Levi. How's it going?"

I told him my situation and I asked for his advice.

"I have an idea, but let me make a couple calls first," he said.

Within a day, everything came together. Parker knew a couple that had been like spiritual parents to him and many others. They were more than willing to help me out by letting me live with them and finish high school in their school district, which required fewer credits than my total. Problem solved.

I stopped by to see Ms. Boyden first thing the next morning. When I told her I would be moving and why, her eyes filled with tears, and she once again hugged me.

"I'm so proud of you, Levi." Her arms were wrapped tightly around me. "You're one resilient kiddo. I am going to miss you!" She really was a great stand-in mom. She even took care of all the paperwork and phone calls needed to get me transferred to the new school for the next week.

On my last day at South, Ms. Boyden called me to her office, and we laughed about our days together. We had walked through many battles in a year and a half.

"Hey, let's go get a soda." She grabbed her purse, and we made for the cafeteria.

When we turned the corner into the lunchroom, I spotted Officer Chapman, Jon the custodian, all my teachers, and a few of my closest friends. They stood around a table piled with cards, a few gifts, and an ice cream cake. I stopped and looked to Ms. Boyden. Her eyes were bright, and a tear slid down her cheek. She urged me forward.

"Go on, Levi, this is for you!"

I never could have guessed in all my days that I really mattered to anyone, but here they all were throwing a surprise party for me.

The cake had four large candles on it that, they said, represented the future, and was covered with camouflage icing—the generous gift of the kitchen staff.

We sat and laughed, sharing stories and putting away the high-calorie treat. Then Ms. Boyden pulled out the last gift. I scanned it, wondering what it could be. When I opened it, my eyes filled with tears yet again. Inside the slim box was a copy of *Oh, the Places You'll Go!* by Dr. Seuss.

I was speechless.

On each inner cover were notes from my teachers and friends, everything from funny memories to well wishes—a memento about not giving up, no matter what. And folded in the center of the book was a newspaper article dated the previous spring, about a local kid who had run away, was homeless, but continued on with high school. Me.

"Turns out we weren't the only ones rooting for you, kid," Ms. Boyden said, smiling and hugging me.

⸺⸺

Ms. Boyden and I walked outside right as school was letting out. We stopped a few steps into the parking lot so she could latch on for another hug.

"Levi, words can't describe how proud I am of you." She was choking up again. "Just promise me you won't try to be a hero too much. That means take care of yourself, okay?"

We both smiled.

Parker was sitting on the hood of his car drinking a Gatorade when we reached him. Ms. Boyden introduced herself.

"You take care of this boy for me, will you, Parker?"

Parker looked at me while I threw my backpack onto the seat of his car. "Yeah, I think I can do that. But he seems to be doing a fine job on his own."

Ms. Boyden grabbed me again and sniffled and squeezed. "I am always here for you, kiddo. I mean that ... always!" She let go and walked back to the building, offering one last good-bye wave before going inside.

Parker playfully elbowed me. "Well li'l bro, you ready to go write the next chapter of your life?"

I smiled, looking back over the school ever so briefly. "Yeah. I'm ready."

"Sweeeet." Parker tossed me the keys to his ride. "You got the wheel."

⁓⁓⁓

I had the wheel. The future, for the first time in my entire life, looked bright. And if I was going to write my future, I was making it a good one!

20

RELENTLESS

Sometimes life throws a detour our way. When it does, we can't give up. Detours aren't dead ends; they just mean we can't get where we want to be from where we are.

We have to find another way, or we won't taste our hopes and dreams.

Many times in my life I hit roadblock after roadblock. And it finally felt like I was getting where I always wanted to go, and along the way I made a few friends who would help me get there.

⸺

I turned off the rattling engine of Parker's old Nissan. We climbed out and headed up the path to the brick house. On the other side of this wall was my new temporary home. When we reached the front door, Parker turned the knob and walked right in. I gave him a *you've got to be kidding me* look.

"What?" he asked innocently, motioning me in. "Man, this is like my home away from home."

I had just cleared the threshold when a man as big as a bear came around the corner and scooped me clean off the ground in a hug. A deep laugh vibrated throughout the house.

"You must be Levi!" the man thundered with his deep chuckle. "Welcome to my humble abode, young'un. If it's mine, it's yours."

Ted Rosetta stood at least six foot six, and not only was he ridiculously tall, he was solid as a sycamore tree. Had he been a hairy man and out in the woods, someone might mistake him for Bigfoot or a bear. But if he *was* a bear, he was more soft teddy than grizzly. Ted was the gentlest of souls. Still, I wouldn't pick a fight with him.

While most grown men I had been around in my life seasoned their speech with four-letter adjectives, Ted was a polar opposite, often laughing with everything he said. It was almost impossible to be around him and not feel like everything would turn out right.

"Oh, you." Ted's wife, Vicki, had come out of the kitchen and grabbed one of his hands to pry me loose. "Put him down already. You're going to scare the poor kid away."

Parker was already sitting in a chair, his face red from laughter.

"You'll have to forgive my husband." Vicki was a tough woman, full of pioneer grit that could weather any storm. When she spoke, you came away realizing you had just listened to someone profoundly wise. But she wasn't one to judge. Vicki just called it like she saw it, and she was often spot on. "Sometimes Ted is a bit too passionate and loving," Vicki said, and shot him a look.

I grinned at both of them. *Yup, I think I am in good hands.*

Ted and Vicki were empty nesters, having sent their only child off to college years ago. Cresting middle age, they were vibrant people, and their hearts overflowed with love and gracious wisdom. Each night was a blessing as we shared a home-cooked meal together.

While I came to them under the assumption I was there to mind my own business, finish school, and head off to the army and war, I never in my wildest dreams expected to taste the life I had always longed for!

And it was a life I could get used to.

<hr>

My move into the Rosettas' was the third week of February, and it was the start of my third high school. I kept my head down. It was sort of pointless to make new friends for the few weeks before school's end, and between being babysat by Sergeant Wolcowitz and spending time with the Rosettas, I was plenty busy.

I did okay there, and graduation day came up fast. I had made it!

The day of the ceremony was awkward. The other kids knew each other, and they laughed and teased friends as everyone lined up. I wanted to put the dorky ceremony behind me and move on with life. The next day, I would be shipping out for basic training.

I waited my turn in line, then crossed the stage and received my diploma. As soon as I stepped off the stage, *bloomf!* a bright flash came from where parents stood taking pictures, and it was timed right as I passed by.

I turned to see who it was. Parker and the Rosettas were somewhere in the audience, but I hadn't asked them to take pictures. Someone called my name from the heavy crowd, but the next student was right behind me, and I couldn't really stop.

As my eyes started to readjust, I saw the back of an elderly man as he merged into the crowd.

Wait ... that can't be. "Harold!" I yelled through the crowd. I tried to hop the privacy rope and walk down an aisle of seats but was quickly discouraged and rerouted by one of the ushers.

That has to be him.

Now the ceremony couldn't end any sooner. How many names could there be after Shepherd? I didn't even bother with the whole hat-tossing thing. Hats rained down around me as I tore into the main aisle, pushing past kids in search of my grandpa—at least I thought that had been him.

Oddly, I didn't even see Parker and the Rosettas where they had been sitting before I'd gone up on stage. I kept searching and waited inside the building until the crowd thinned enough so I knew they weren't there. Finally, I walked out of the large auditorium doors. Standing off to the side of the veranda stood Parker and the Rosettas, Ms. Boyden, Jon, and Officer Chapman. Parker held a poster board that said, "Way to go, Levi! We are so proud of you!" I laughed and walked toward them, scanning the crowd exiting the building just in case. Then Parker stepped aside, and coming from behind Jon was ...

My Grandpa Harold.

I paused to swallow the lump in my throat, and my hands began shaking. It was really him!

I shot across the short distance and slowed just enough so as not to tackle the man I dearly loved. He threw his arms around me and we both wept.

"I am so proud," his voice quivered in my ear. "So proud of you."

We stood hugging each other and crying.

I had been so hyperfocused on getting ready for the army, I had forgotten to call Ms. Boyden. Good thing Parker was on top of things. Ms. Boyden made sure Officer Chapman tracked down my grandpa and gave him the graduation details.

Harold had barely released me when Ms. Boyden scooted in for one of her famous motherly hugs. "You did it, kiddo." Her mascara was streaking on her face. "I always knew you would!"

⁓

Under a cloudless, star-filled sky that night, we celebrated and shared a few laughs. The finishing touch to what had been a rough childhood. And never in all my days could I have imagined spending it with such inspiring people.

With one last hoorah, I rode off into the sunset and into the army to live out my hopes and dreams.

Time to go be all that I could be.

21

WHO NEEDS SLEEP?

Wait ... wait ... *wait!*

Shouldn't we stop just for a second and smell the roses? Maybe look around for once and enjoy ourselves? Life is short, *too* short, and if you don't look around once in a while it will pass you by.

Then there is no getting it back.

Maybe this is the only way we can live without regrets—by *seizing the day* or the moment. Whatever you choose to call it.

I should heed my own advice on that one. I still have trouble figuring out if seizing the day is smelling the roses or pursuing my goals.

For most of my life I didn't want to stop and look around, because the stuff around me twisted my gut with anxiety. Due to that, I learned a bad habit: keep my eyes forward, keep pushing forward. I couldn't even tell you what roses smelled like. The unfortunate consequence was that I rarely stopped to enjoy myself, even when I was experiencing love for the first time.

I should have stopped.

My last day as a civilian I spent in the company of the tender-hearted Rosettas. Parker had come over, and we all sat at the kitchen table and enjoyed a gourmet, home-cooked meal. Then, with daylight nearing its end, the Rosettas and I took off for Sergeant Wolcowitz's office.

The three of us stood outside on the parking lot. Ted leaned down for one of his scoop-you-up bear hugs. Vicki peeled him off and hugged me herself, her eyes overflowing.

"Remember, Levi, wherever you go, no matter how bad it gets around you, remember God is always right there with you!"

I stepped back from her hug. "Thank you guys so much for everything."

With our good-byes said and a few tears shed, I stepped into the recruiting office.

"Well, Shepherd"—Sergeant Wolcowitz came out of the commode and noticed me standing there—"you ready to do this?"

"Sure am, Sergeant." I shot him a smile. "Let's roll."

After a few pieces of last-minute paperwork and a short drive, we arrived at the airport Holiday Inn. We walked into the overly air-conditioned lobby.

"Son, you're going to do just fine in this army." He looked at me square on. "You have a grit and tenacity that can't be taught, and if you use those to your advantage, you will do great things. And, who knows, maybe someday I'll be saluting you!"

I shook his outstretched hand. "Thank you, Sergeant. I will give my best."

⌒⌒⌒

The elevator stopped as I headed up to my room, and another young man my age stepped on. He thumped a button on the control panel. I could tell by his luggage he was shipping out, too.

"'Sup, man." I stuck my hand out. "I'm Levi. Where you shipping out to?"

"Chris Bishop." His voice was a bit hoarse, and he smelled like a hangover. "Benning. You?"

"The same." I smiled. "Eleven Bravo. You?"

"For sure."

Chris was going to be a grunt like me. He kind of fit the psychiatric profile, too: intense personality, foul-mouthed. He swayed and steadied himself against the elevator wall. "Last night of freedom, man," he said, taking a drink from a water bottle. "One last hoorah before they own you, you know?"

Bishop was a natural comedian, able to make a joke out of almost any situation. We hung out together for the rest of the night and enjoyed a free meal, compliments of the hotel. We managed a swim before it was lights out. Even on our last night, the hotel put the dozen or so of us on an eleven o'clock curfew.

The early bedtime didn't help. Sleep avoided me. I couldn't stop thinking about the days to come, and I lay awake thinking about what combat would be like. We already had boots on the ground in Afghanistan, and rumors spoke of going into Iraq as well.

What kind of man would I be when the bullets started to fly? Could anyone really know until the first fool shoots at you—and misses? And if he didn't miss, well … I didn't fear dying in combat.

I lay staring at the ceiling until the front desk gave me the four o'clock wake-up call.

After a quick buffet breakfast and a bus ride to the enlistment center, we boarded a flight out of Kansas City International bound for Atlanta. Bishop and I were on our way to Fort Benning, Georgia.

We arrived at the base at two o'clock in the morning—0200 hours. As soon as we had gotten off the coach bus that ferried a dozen of us from Atlanta, a man dressed in BDUs and a drill sergeant's wide-brimmed hat came striding up to us.

"Get your puny hides …"—spit showered from his mouth as he got in the face of one of the nameless boys from the bus—"… in the front lean and rest position. Now!"

The army has a different way of saying almost everything, and this was his fancy way of saying a push-up position.

This was the beginning—a relentless process of being broken of our individuality and being rebuilt as *one*. Drill sergeants are experts in this, and ours left us there for twenty minutes or more, long past the point when every muscle quakes in fatigue. It took all I had to keep my face out of the dirt.

When we were finally allowed to stand, we all hurt, but pain was a part of the process. Pain speeds it up. We filed into a line, were given a small meal of rubber eggs, bacon, and grits—obviously leftovers from yesterday's breakfast—and then were led to barracks and issued blankets to make up the bare bunks.

The drill sergeant left us with his kind words. "Better get some sleep, ladies." He stood at the doorway and flicked off the lights.

"Wake-up is at 0400." The sergeant laughed. "Oh, and by the way, it's 0355 now. Goodnight!"

Well at least we get five minutes of sleep. Good thing he couldn't hear the sarcasm in my mind, because that would have cost me. But this is what I signed up for.

Welcome to the US Army.

22

CONTRABAND KINGS

Who are you? Who am I?

None of that mattered anymore. Not in the army. Once enlisted, you are no longer an independent person. You become part of a larger force. A soldier, one in many—part of a war machine dedicated to doing your nation's dirty work.

For those of us who were infantry, *grunts*, that identity drives down even deeper. In the infantry, you are brothers, you live together, you fight together and, if the hour comes, *you die together*.

⁓

Those days, weeks, and months of training were physically and emotionally grueling. When I look back on them now, they flew by too quickly. Each passing moment gave way to the conviction that I belonged. I had always felt like a drifter in life, but I found my purpose and self-worth with the men I served alongside, with boys who later, in wars far away, would fight and die like men. They were the most genuine family I had ever known, and I loved them and every minute of it.

I was made for it.

The second day on base, I stood in line at the reception battalion's barber, waiting for my standard-issue buzz cut. Really, it was more of a scalping, with your head shaved down to the pink skin, which had never seen the light of day.

I felt a tap on the shoulder, and a voice behind me whispered, "Hey, man, you think they gonna let me keep my 'fro?"

A few drill sergeants patrolled the line ever so often, so I glanced furtively behind me. There stood a tall, lanky, light-skinned African

American, with dark freckles strewn across the bridge of his nose and cheeks.

"Name's Quinton White." He leaned forward, still keeping his voice hushed. "I got your back—for real." We both held back a laugh.

Quinton White was about my age, and although his posture matched the rest of us, I could tell he didn't have a serious bone in his body. He also had one of the most rocking retro afros I'd ever seen, even on old disco movies.

During basic, he and I were paired up as battle buddies, the army's term for the soldier you are assigned to for every activity. In our platoon, everyone gave each other nicknames. Quinton's was "Q-Tip," based on his silhouette when he first arrived at basic. Being a black man with the last name *White* didn't help either.

White and I became best friends, kindred spirits too rowdy to tame, too stubborn to quiet, and wickedly street smart. Survivors. And we shared some memorable times.

One was to stack the fire watch (nightly guard duty) in our barracks during basic with a few guys we knew would keep their mouths shut. An hour after everyone in the barracks nodded off, White and I would sneak out past the guard on watch and down the road to the mess hall. White's father was a locksmith, so he knew how to pick a lock. After filling a few canteens full of Powerade from the soda fountain and liberating a few Choco Tacos from the freezer, we'd bang out of there. As trainees, we were never allowed to have these items, but they were strategically placed in the mess hall so we'd have to pass by temptingly close at every meal. Whatever we didn't consume while ducking and dodging through the tree line along the road, we'd sell off to the highest bidder when we got back. Our little clandestine missions happened a lot more than I should admit.

White and I were the contraband kings during our days at basic. He had my back and I had his, and whatever came our way, we would go down swinging *together*.

⸻

After a week of monotony at the reception battalion, we moved to our training barracks. On our first day, we stood rank and file in the parking lot, waiting to meet our full-time drill instructors, Sergeants Bullock and Long.

These were the men who would train Oscar platoon, my platoon. Both men were combat veterans and cycled in and out as Ranger instructors during the course of their army careers.

Sergeant Long, a short black man with a mean streak, was the vocal one, vocal *beyond* the stereotypical potty mouth of a drill sergeant. And while his mouth was loud, it was also flashy—several of his teeth were crowned with gold, making him an expensive trash talker. Sometimes he'd say something so hilariously wrong—and this was while he was being serious—we'd laugh hard enough that tears streamed down our cheeks. Of course, that only got us more pain—in the *front lean and rest position.*

He was a man you couldn't help respect, not because of the title he held, but because of where he had been in the army. Sgt. Tyrone Long was a veteran of Operation Just Cause (Panama) and Desert Shield and Desert Storm (the First Gulf War). The man knew what he was talking about when it came to being a warrior.

Our other instructor, Sgt. Michael Bullock, was a soldier through and through, with a weathered soul and muscles like solid rock. Though average height, his very presence was intimidating, because you knew *he* knew every way in the book to kill a man. You didn't cross him.

Like Sergeant Long, Sergeant Bullock had served in Operations Desert Shield and Desert Storm. But Sergeant Bullock had also served in Operation Gothic Serpent (the Rangers' operation in Mogadishu, Somalia), and for that he was a celebrity on base. The movie *Black Hawk Down* had come out three months prior to our time together. The movie was a Hollywood reenactment of the battle of Mogadishu, in which about 5,000 enemy combatants ambushed 140 American troops. Two American helicopters were shot down, and 18 American soldiers were killed. And we all know you never leave a man behind.

During the engagement, Sergeant Bullock, then almost a decade younger, went back into the embattled city on foot with a shock team of Delta operators. They fought their way back to the surrounded Rangers who were protecting each of the downed choppers. When a hotshot Hollywood producer asked him for permission to use his name and depict his courage in battle, he told them to shove it. He wanted neither fame nor recognition. "You fight like hell for the man next to you," were words he would often echo to us, engraining that mentality deep in our psyche. "One way, we all come home together, even if it's carried by your brothers, draped in the stars and stripes."

I take great pride in the fact that the man who taught me how to wage war had proven himself without question.

We stood in formation that day, watching as they approached us for the first time. Sergeant Bullock was the first to look over our crop of new recruits. As he assessed each one of us, his eyes stopped on me and scanned over my nametape, his lips forming my last name silently. His eyes lit up, and he pushed past the first rank of my platoon and steamed right to me, stopping inches from my face.

"Who do you think you are"—his spit showered my face—"wearing your rank like you think you're somebody!"

I was a newbie like all the rest, but I was one of a few who had already earned the rank of Private First Class before basic, and that meant I was either *gung ho* and had earned my rank, or I was a brown nose. And I was no brown nose. Now was not the time to advertise my ambitions.

"Private..." he hesitated, leaning back to be more dramatic. "*Excuse* me, Private *First Class* Shepherd—you don't know the first thing about being a soldier, and you can wear that rank when I say you've earned it." With swift yanks, he tore both insignias from my BDU shirt collar. "Get in the front lean and rest position—*now!*"

I dropped to the deck without a word, and hovered, staring at the sandy dirt of southern Georgia.

"Son, a man you call a friend ratted you out." He knelt, his face so close to mine I could tell he'd had a cup of coffee before heading to our formation. "He wanted to ask me for a small favor. Seems you're a little tough guy with a past. You've had quite a life, kid. Let's see just how much determination you've really got!"

That "friend" had been Sergeant Wolcowitz, and the favor was to keep me in line. But Sergeant Wolcowitz's *passion* didn't end there. I found out later he'd faxed Sergeant Bullock a CliffsNotes version of my life: the cancer, Ozanam, my runaway days, the failed drug test—anything that'd give ammo to a man who took great delight in breaking the human psyche so it could be rebuilt stronger.

"Private, if you think you have earned the right to attend my Ranger school by proving yourself to some hotshot Spec Ops boy, you don't know a thing about nothing. I am going to ride you so hard, you'll wish you were dead."

Sergeant Bullock then ordered the platoon to another area, but he never told me to stand from the push-up position. I was left there to feel the burn of muscle fatigue.

Drill Sergeant Bullock wandered by about an hour into it. I was long since shifting positions, using every angle possible that was allowed as long as my stomach didn't touch the ground, or I didn't stand up. My whole body trembled violently with an unimaginable burn. Sergeant Bullock set a tray of hot chow and a bottle of Gatorade within sight. The smell of the food wafted my way, and the cold bottle glistened with sweat beads in the sun.

"Hey, boy." He looked at me, as he mockingly knelt and smelled the food. "I bet you are hungry, thirsty, and *hurting!* Question is, do you want to quit yet and go home?"

"N-o … Dr-il-l Ser-geant." My voice shook along with my muscles.

"No you don't want to quit? Or no you don't want to go home?" He leaned on one knee and put a wad of chew under his lip, flicking the rest of his finger into the dirt in front of me. "Oh, that's right; you don't have a home. Nobody wanted you. That makes you an *orphan*, doesn't it?"

I eased into a pyramid to speak clearly. "No … I … don't quit!"

Sergeant Bullock stood, spitting a wad of rancid-smelling dip on the ground beneath my face. "We'll see about that." And he walked away.

Not long after that, I collapsed into a heap of exhaustion and face-planted into his smelly spit. But I had his attention for all the wrong reasons, and he rode my hide relentlessly all through basic, so much so that many in my platoon teased me about being the "teacher's pet."

His motto was: "What doesn't kill you makes you stronger." I feared I was his test case.

Basic training came and went in the blink of an eye, and now came the time for five weeks of AIT (Advanced Individual Training) for us in Eleven Bravo. Five weeks of Infantry School, learning the fine art of waging war on the ground. Fort Benning was an OSUT (One Station Unit Training) base, so that meant that for unit cohesiveness and training, all infantrymen were kept together from basic through AIT, up until the point of being sent to our assigned Infantry Division.

For those of us being sent to RIP (Ranger Indoctrination Program, now called RASP, Ranger Assessment Selection Program), we would have to go through three weeks of Basic Airborne Course before being rolled into the Ranger Training Brigade for selection. If we passed selection, we were sent to one of the three remaining Ranger Battalions (the First, Second, and Third Ranger Battalions). If we washed out or quit selection, we would be sent to the Eighty-second Airborne Division up at Fort Bragg. Either way, we were Airborne Infantry, one notch above a regular grunt, and one step closer to being one of the finest infantrymen to ever patrol this earth.

Since Fort Benning was an OSUT, we had the fine distinction of having our drill sergeants follow us into Infantry School. Thankfully, Sergeant Bullock was no longer determined to kill me. I must have proven myself to him, and he'd eased up enough so he actually came off as legitimately nice, almost like a friend—if that's possible for someone without a heart.

At the end of Infantry School, we were all awarded the honor of the Turning Blue ceremony, a dedication when all infantrymen are awarded their baby blue Infantry Cord, distinctly braided around the right shoulder on the dress uniform of an infantryman.

Most of the other men I'd come to recognize during the months of training were heading out to their infantry divisions across the globe, but everyone in my company was staying behind at Fort Benning for Airborne school, with half going to the Eighty-second Airborne afterwards, and the rest being rolled into the Ranger Training Brigade.

Of all the men I served with that summer, nine would later pay the ultimate sacrifice in service of our country. One was famous: Corporal Patrick Tillman, an NFL football player who chose honor over money. The others are men whose names you will never hear in the news, that are gone but never forgotten, and one is a man whose name I will always carry close to my heart.

Private Quinton "Q-Tip" White was killed in action April 8, 2004, in Afghanistan, while serving in the Third Ranger Battalion.

Some men sit and whine about things they never had the courage to fight for, while others put it all on the line and stand for their beliefs. This is what separates the boys from the men, even if those men happen to still be boys when their days on this earth come to an end.

23

CALLING GRAVITY'S BLUFF

Some do not walk through life; rather they run, and set a standard for us all.

Others look back from their deathbed, and regret a life that never was. Still others are lost too soon, but they go down swinging in a blaze of glory.

Life is seldom what we imagine it to be, but it is *exactly* what we make of it with the time given. Some understand and push ahead; others never seem to grasp this concept and suffer a lifetime of regrets.

What will we do with the time we are given?

Each one of us will answer this eternal question differently, but nonetheless, it's one we will all have to account for in our final moments.

⌐⌐

For me, it was neither the time to walk nor run, but to fly—literally! I was off into the sky. My days of being a *leg* were over.

I was a paratrooper.

After months of training in my army career, I was now in airborne training at BAC (Basic Airborne Course) at Fort Benning, a school where they teach soldiers how to jump out of a perfectly good airplane, not only as a means of troop deployment, but as a requirement to advance to the next level and be elite.

And every course I took was one step closer to my goal.

It was early September 2002. I was still at Fort Benning, Georgia, and would be for weeks to come in Ranger Training, where I'd either prove myself as a Ranger, or be sent back to the Eighty-second Airborne as a regular paratrooper.

If I stood to the end, I would be the best—with the *tab* and *scroll* to prove it.

Airborne training is a hectic schedule of fast-paced, endless classes, run-throughs, and mock-ups. First, we trained on the ground, both in the classroom, then on a dummy plane raised a dozen feet off the ground. Then, we transitioned to the jump towers, a pair of three-hundred-foot steel structures where we would be dropped in a full parachute harness suspended from a steel skeleton-framed parachute. It gave us a taste of a controlled free fall.

When we finally finished the ground exercises, it was time to take the training wheels off and earn our jump wings. This meant five live jumps from an Air Force Hercules C-130 at thirteen hundred feet.

Our jumpmasters pounded us with the facts: simulations are nothing; you need to taste the real thing to understand; gravity is a liar—time to call her bluff.

On the first trip up, after the macho bravado curbed a bit, there was an eerie silence as our jump time neared. Everyone was probably thinking the same thing as I was: Why did I volunteer for this again?

Maybe it was out of ignorance, or maybe it was for honor. The reason for being in this airplane didn't matter to the meal doing somersaults in your stomach and calling you a *fool*.

The first jump passed in a blur of shouted orders, wind, panic, weightlessness, a sharp jerk, and then a rolling landing. Flushed with adrenaline after one jump, we took a few hours to review in class and eat a meal, and then it was off to the airfield again for a second jump and an encore adrenaline rush.

By the third jump, we were veterans of the sky. We chatted on the climb to altitude, joked about who could perform the best landing, and vowed to take up skydiving during our free time—once we had any.

The fourth jump was at night, and our jumpmasters reminded us to watch for ground obstacles when landing. An injury—in the real world—could take a man out of the fight, and that might jeopardize an entire mission.

I know the C-130 was probably just as loud as ever, but the darkness seemed to mute the roaring engines and jangling gear. And when we jumped, the silent beauty stole my breath. Dozens of soldiers filled the sky, each a falling star marked by an attached chem-glo stick. The way the moonlight glinted off the inflated nylon canopies made it appear as if the sky were filled with Portuguese man-o-war, jellyfish-like creatures with powerful, dreadfully painful stings.

We may not have been creatures of the sea, but we were most definitely *men of war.*

⸺⸻

I had one last jump to go as an airborne cadet, and then I was off to Colonel Darby's playground, the nickname for the Ranger training obstacle course at Fort Benning. It was a stunning, cloudless day, and the temperature was mild for a late summer afternoon in the Deep South.

We lined up on the tarmac, waiting to board the aircraft. Like every time before, we checked and double-checked our equipment before being rechecked and marked off by one of the jumpmasters. With a high-pitched whine of hydraulics, the empty Hercules lowered her ramp, yielding entrance to the cargo bay.

Excitement coursed through my veins, and I joined the fist-bumping bravado with the men around me. One by one, we all checked with the loadmaster, and I took one last look at the gorgeous day around me before climbing the ramp to my canvas strap seat. All around me, men pulled harnesses down, securing themselves for what was always a steep and bumpy takeoff.

I leaned back in my harness while chomping on a piece of gum, trying to get my mind right for the jump. The excess adrenaline was causing my heart to pound away in my throat. As usual, I had to wipe away the sweat that beaded on my palms, so I nonchalantly adjusted my weapons case that was strapped between my knees, wiping my hands on the coarse surface with one smooth motion.

The final seconds of our grounding drew near, and the thunderous yet restrained growl of the four massive propeller engines vibrated the fuselage of the craft. Then the C-130 began taxiing, twisting through a few turns before stopping ever so briefly at the end of the runway.

The engines wound up, glorified by their release to do what they were created for. The aircraft lurched forward, listing all of us in the cargo hold to the rear as we launched down the tarmac. In seconds, the tires left the ground and the plane angled to what felt to be straight up. I did my best to fight down the bile that shot into my throat, and hoped the pilots weren't trainees like *I* was.

As steep as the ascent had been, it felt like we were diving when the pilots suddenly pushed over and our bodies floated against the straps in weightlessness. Then the plane leveled off and I concluded the pilots *were*, in fact, trainees. Or idiots.

Being that Fryar Drop Zone was not too far away, the training flights were always short. I joined in with those seated around me as we cracked raunchy jokes and made small talk. "Yo, Shep, you ready to go drop the Talis or what?" Private Cahill shouted from a few seats away.

"For sure, man," I shouted back so he could hear over the white noise of the aircraft. "Just get me over there, you know?"

The plane banked a couple of times, and the indicator at the head of the cargo hold lit up red, which meant we were approaching our drop zone.

At the front of the hold, the senior jumpmaster used hand signals along with his words to make sure we understood.

"Airborne! Stand up, hook up!"

In unison, all of us unfastened our seat harnesses and stood, stacking up along the two aisles that ran along the cargo hold.

I fumbled for the yellow static line that was secured over my shoulder, brought it to the anchor line atop the fuselage, and snapped the carabineer firmly into place. The hold echoed with the sound of metal on metal, dozens of troopers doing the same.

I made a loop—a bight—in my static line so I could slide it along the anchor line as I walked. I was good to go.

One by one, each trooper sounded off along the line, letting the jumpmaster know they were ready to jump.

The jumpmaster hit the control that opened the two side doors of the C-130, and wind surged through the hold, mixing the smell of sweaty men and hydraulic fuel with fresh ozone from the sky outside.

My eyes focused on the front of the hold. A buzzer sounded, and the indicator light turned green. We were over our drop zone.

"Go! Go! Go!" the jumpmaster shouted above the rushing wind.

No matter how brave you force your mind to be, your body realizes the foolishness of what you're about to do. Your sympathetic nervous system shoots a burst of *fight or flight* into your bloodstream, and you can feel that twinge in your abdomen as your heart races and your senses slow.

One by one, each soldier stepped up to the door and jumped. In one instant he was there, and the next he wasn't, vanishing into thin air.

Private White was two men ahead of me. Jokester that he was, he shouted at the jumpmaster, "If my mama knew you were making me do this, she'd give you a whoopin.'"

"Ya don't say?" The jumpmaster smiled, acting hurt as he took the bight loop from White. "Now get off my airplane!"

White jumped, as did the men behind him. I was up.

I handed the jumpmaster the bight of my static line and moved to the edge of the door, gripping the frame with my hands. I paused to take in the tranquil scene of the earth rushing far below.

I threw up a peace sign at the jumpmaster. Then, without hesitation, I stepped into the sky.

24

BROKEN MASTERPIECE

I guess some things are never meant to be. We watch as everything we have longed for, strived for, runs though our grasp like a strip of 550-paracord risers tethered to a parachute caught by a gust of wind at the drop zone. Sometimes the elements of life are stronger than we are, and we get drug along for the ride until we learn to let go.

You're probably saying to yourself, "Oh no, not again. I thought this was a book about God, redemption, and hope?"

Oh, it is. Believe me, it is.

Sometimes, though, God waits until all the pieces are out of our hands—broken beyond *our* ability to repair them—before he puts *his* masterpiece together.

Believe me, he will come through.

⸻

I'd gotten beat up on that last jump, but that was beside the point. I sat on the edge of my bed facing an officer who'd come by to deliver more than just my Jump Wings and Airborne Tab.

Major, an officer whose name tape eluded me, handed me a dossier with my name plastered all over it. "Here, Private. I need you to sign these."

I opened it up. The top sheet starred back at me causing my heart to move into my throat. It read *Honorable/Medical Discharge*. "Sir, what it this?" my voice cracked with emotion.

"I'm sorry, son. I know how bad you want this, but my hands are tied. You just can't serve with these kinds of medical issues." No man ever wants to crush the dreams of another, and he stood motionless creating the aura of compassion. I was in no rush to sign it, and I am sure he was aware of that. "I know this is the last thing you were expecting. Believe me, if there was something I could do, I would."

The pen convulsed in my hand, or maybe it was the other way around. I brought my head up as my eyes moistened. I looked the major in the eyes as I signed the papers, effectively discharging me from the US Army. I was deemed physically unfit for service, for combat, and I was no use to the army any more. There'd be no hope of rehab, nor a desk job.

Over. The end.

I was never naive to the fact that as an infantryman I was expendable. I just didn't realize that also meant disposable

The major took the documents and offered his hand in respect just before leaving the room. "I'm sorry, Levi."

One moment he called me by my rank, as a proud solider. The next I was just a man again, a civilian called by his given name. I can't say I blame them. I'd gotten roughed up just days earlier, and while I was at medical on the mend, a mixture of the present injuries and my past medical issues, having had cancer, came calling.

And while the rest of my brothers marched onto Ranger selection, I sat in a room starring out the window with a thousand-yard stare. Over the next week several men who had become like blood to me swung by to say good-bye before going to their next duty stops. I even got a call from Sergeant Wolcowitz, and it was filled with well-wishes and apologies. Part of the blame lay at his feet. He had never told me that my previous cancer status would exclude me from service, nor did he include those details in my enlistment documents. He just saw a man who could fight and a man who could lead, and he wanted to help. How could I blame him? He had helped mold me into a man.

My last night on base Sergeant Bullock came by. He had made it his mission to check on me every night on his way home, even though I was in the opposite direction. But the two of us had become friends-of-sorts.

While the other nights had held some tears—well, *my* tears because drill sergeants don't cry—and some very salty jokes, tonight was different.

He was never a man of long winded speeches, and when he entered the room, he reached down into the cargo pockets of his BDUs and pulled out a pair of Choco Tacos and Powerades—a silent recognition that he was not ignorant of the mischief White and I reigned back in basic training. Maybe it was an unspoken way of apologizing for being so hard on me.

When our window of time came to an end, he stood and set his posture with the authority I had known in basic.

"Shepherd, I have had the honor of serving and training with some of the best this nation has ever seen. Some men just have it, others don't. It's not something you can choose—it's in the heart."

His eyes focused on a place far from this room, in his memories past, and his eyes misted a bit. "If I was ever surrounded again by more enemies than I had bullets for, you are one man I'd want with me in that fight!"

Sergeant Bullock took a step forward as he slid his utility knife from its sheath. In a smooth motion, he cut the Ranger Tab off his BDU and set it in my hand, held in place by his firm handshake.

"It doesn't take a course to make a ranger; it takes a course to tell us who the rangers are!"

Both of us had moist eyes, and before either of us said a word, he nodded his head and left the room.

My dream, the US Army, was finished.

The army was all I had wanted, all I had planned for, and now I was left almost back where I started, and I didn't know what to do or where to go. I had no backup plan.

The next morning I stood by a pay phone, my palms sweating, as I forced myself to pick up the handset and call the only person I knew who could help me make sense of this mess. The song "Where Are You Going" by the Dave Matthew's Band came on the radio in the lobby, its words echoing through the near-empty room.

The singer was asking where I was going, what I was looking for. I had no answer. Nor did I know what I was really looking for. What I thought I wanted had been forcibly snatched out of my hands.

Then the lyrics spoke of resting with "me" until I was okay again. Where *was* I going? I had nowhere left to go.

As the call connected, Parker's voice came on the line, groggy from the earliness of the hour. "Hello?"

"Hey, man, it's me. I'm …" My throat constricted as I fought back tears.

"Levi. You all right?" His voice perked up a bit more as he recognized me.

"Yeah, I'm okay. Parker, they"—I broke into a sob—"they're sending me home. I guess I'm …"

I was broken—and I couldn't even finish my sentence. I was trying to say I was coming home, but that was just it—I thought the army and my brothers were my home.

"Levi, you're okay man. We're here for you. Tell you what, make your way back to KC, and we'll take care of you."

Kansas City. Parker's logic made sense, and that was the only place I had left to turn. Parker and the Rosettas had known I was injured in the jump, but none of them knew I would be coming home, not until now, and they were willing to drop everything and run to me, to let my hurt be theirs.

Parker and I ended our conversation. I took a taxi to the Greyhound station in old-town Columbus, Georgia, and boarded the transport back to my hometown.

A town filled with a lifetime of painful memories.

A little over twenty-four hours later, the Greyhound's airbrakes squealed to a stop in downtown Kansas City, and I hobbled off the bus. The midday sun reflected blindingly off the skyscrapers of the metropolis, and I shielded my sleep-deprived eyes as I walked toward the bus station.

I spotted a makeshift cardboard sign that said, "Welcome home, young'un." A mountainous Ted Rosetta stood behind the sign, dressed in his old-school flannel shirt and jeans.

We saw each other at the same time, and he came forward in a hurried shuffle. I let him come since I sure wasn't going anywhere fast. The selfless man that he was, he grabbed my military duffle bag off my right shoulder and gave me a careful hug.

His hug felt safe in a hard and unforgiving world. If there was one man who could comfort a hurting soul, it was Ted Rosetta.

We rode in his coffee-fragranced car for home. Ted never once during the ride asked how I felt. To do so would have been like pouring alcohol in an open wound. No, he kept the conversation lighthearted, even cracked jokes, and we laughed together. I felt the weight of my burden lighten a little. Besides, he didn't need to ask how I felt; he already knew.

And the bucket of Popeyes chicken he had resting between us on the front seat sure hit the spot.

Ted angled the car into the drive and parked, then came around to my side to help me out.

"Levi, you sure look different from the last time I saw you." He paused, gave me a head-to-toe once-over, and let out a deep, worried sigh. "You've been to hell and back. I'm sorry, son." He put his arms around me but restrained himself from lifting me off the ground like he used to. It took everything I had not to break down into a full-blown sobfest as I put my arms around him.

After a few moments, Ted helped me up the steps to the apartment they had built over their garage. He shot me a look that was worth a million words before he disappeared back into the main house below.

I sank into the old La-Z-Boy by the window, leaned back, and kicked up the footrest. As comfortable as this chair was, I longed for my stiff cot in the barracks, where other men snored so loudly the paint flaked off the ceiling, where sergeants screamed in my face about what an idiot I was for some minor infraction, where men would give their life for me and I the same, where I had a family of brothers.

I held it in for as long as I could, long enough to make sure Ted was in the house and occupied, then I broke down into a river of tears.

The dam had breached, and the floodwaters from a life of pain were now surging out of me, destroying all hope in their path. And I was convinced there was only one remedy: hurry up and get it over with.

25

STICKY NOTES

The days of hope had long since abandoned me. If I were to say I had any thoughts of God, it would be a lie.

Whatever thoughts I did have weren't inspiring.

An abyss of ever-widening pain in my soul would soon consume the progress I'd made.

***

Over the next few days, I slept deeply in hibernation mode. The months of intense physical and emotional training had caught up with me. Added to my body's need to heal the soft-tissue damage, the combination made a recipe of near-ceaseless slumber.

After two weeks of sleep, I emerged from my cave atop the garage and made my way downstairs to the house. I decided to look for a job, and Ted lent me the keys to his car so I could go pick my car up out of storage.

***

The Rosettas had a neighbor whose son, Duane, was about my age. He was twenty, a high school dropout, and covered with tattoos. A dyed jet-black Mohawk rode the ridge of his head.

Duane always spoke in a brash voice as if he were shouting, and you could instantly tell why when you saw him pull up in his beat-up pickup, music blaring out of headphones he wore almost everywhere. The noise from those little speakers was loud enough you could make out the words to the song from across the yard.

Not long after I returned to Kansas City, Duane spotted me and came over.

"Hey, man, why you back?" he asked, giving me a chance to tell yet another person why I was home. He listened with a distant look in his eyes, like he didn't really care but wanted to appear concerned nonetheless. "So, you looking for job, I take it?"

Matter of fact, I was, and Duane had the hookup. He worked at a liberal arts college not far from the house and offered to get me on at the college kitchen in the cook-to-order grill below the school's main cafeteria.

I rejoined life as a civilian, working full-time nights and weekends at The Grill at the college, and I found that being a workaholic helped keep my mind off the pain and off the loss of the army.

Ted and Vicki, bless their souls, did everything they could to help, from taking me out to dinner just to talk, to gentle, handwritten Scripture verses on my bed when I came home from work.

Wisdom penned on sticky notes: "God is always at work" and "All things work for good."

Despite the love behind the gesture, those notes were hard to stomach. I didn't want to even think of God, let alone him always at work in my life. To me, if he was on the job, he sure had fallen asleep a long time ago.

Pride is a stupid thing—especially mine. The stronger the Rosettas pursued me, the harder I pushed them away. To those who loved unconditionally, I was quickly becoming a distant, coldhearted jerk. Even while the Rosettas continued their voice of love, another voice appeared, one tempting me to go a different way.

Duane was the face to that voice.

Since he worked upstairs in the cafeteria as a dishwasher, he would routinely come by after my shift and invite me to go party with him. At first I declined, uninterested in anything but returning to my in-law apartment at the Rosettas' and going to bed.

But one night I figured, *why not?* and went with him to his buddy's house. And with no reason to have to wake up until the next afternoon for work, I found that endless booze and weed helped shut up the voices of pain in my own mind—or at least muffle them. After all, I couldn't remember the past if I killed off the brain cells that held those memories. And just like every other addiction under the sun, I needed a little more the next time, and the time after that, and the time after that.

So began my endless search to find anything to shut down my mind. It became all I lived for.

26

CHRONICLES IN THE MAKING

The death of my soul had been a chronicle long in the making, a sad story with seemingly endless encores, each worse than the previous.

Why was I even brought into this cruel world? The people responsible for that decision were long gone, and I was left here to face this hell on my own.

Somewhere, there had to be something or someone who could fix this mess and heal the agony in my soul.

I was determined to find it, though I had a bad habit of looking in all the wrong places. Imagine that.

———

I had been back from the army two months. One night, as usual, Duane came downstairs from work at the cafeteria to invite me to the next party place.

"Hey, partner," Duane practically hollered at me from two feet away, "you want to do me a favor and drive a connection of mine someplace? Dude, I'll drop ya thirty just for taking him a few miles away."

Thirty dollars just for taking some guy across town? That was a no-brainer.

Duane's buddy was a dishwasher upstairs named Glenn, and he was holed up in a motel, lying low from some folks. I made it *my* business not to get in *his* business.

The taxi job was to take Glenn to some guy's house, which I did. I parked my car, and Glenn walked inside. He came out a half hour later, stoned as a caveman. I'd been around crackheads back in the day with my cousin Wyatt, so I knew just what had gone on inside the house. Glenn handed me the thirty as promised, and I took him back to his motel room.

Days later, Glenn came to me himself and asked me to drive to the house again, only this time he wouldn't be going along. The man inside the house wanted to come out and meet me.

When I pulled up, a man was sitting on the front stoop smoking a cigarette. He looked suspiciously down one side of the street, then the other, before coming to my car and getting in. "You Levi?" the man asked, smoke still billowing out of his nostrils like a dragon.

"Yeah." I sat motionlessly. The dude seemed hyped on something, and my read came up *hustler*.

"A'ight." He stuck his hand out for a sideways handshake. "I'm Jay. You need to take me somewheres. If you keep your trap shut, there's a bill waiting for you when we're done."

A bill. $100.

My closer scrutiny saw the signs of a dealer. Faded prison tats rolled all over any piece of visible flesh, and he had cold eyes, flat, like he didn't care about nothing.

Jay had just gotten out of a Texas Supermax a month earlier, having spent the last twenty years on lockdown for dealing, the latest of his prison time. He was serving time before I was even born. The house he'd come out of was his sister's; in fact, he wasn't supposed to be anywhere except Texas. Except Jay played by no one's rules but his own.

The deal was on the other side of Kansas City in the worst part of town, on the Kansas side of the Quindaro. As a white guy, you didn't step foot on that road unless you were *somebody* or a cop.

After that night, those runs with him kept piling up, and so did the cash I made from being his driver. Just like that, I went back to old ways, running with hustlers and thugs. For some reason, I fell in love with the lifestyle and no longer wanted to be a good ol' boy.

One day, while the Rosettas were at work, I got up, packed my things, and left without saying a word. I'd been in their home three months, and all they got was a thank-you and good-bye on a wrinkled piece of paper.

I didn't leave them a forwarding address or phone number. I just left. I hated good-byes, and I learned from my childhood to simply move on to the next place.

I look back and wonder how I could do that to someone I cared about, to people who loved me? It was selfish and ungrateful behavior, but I also knew it would break their hearts if they knew what I was doing.

I leased an apartment across town. And not long after I got my own place, I was fired from the college. One night, Duane and I had gone up to the girls dorm to party, and we were there long after visiting hours. We got busted with beer, lots of it, and none of us were of age.

Now I was in a jam due to my own boneheadedness. I had a new place and no source of income. That was unless…

While looking for a job, I started doing more runs with Jay—anything to keep an eviction notice off my door. Duane and I parted ways after that night in the dorm, but before the bust he'd introduced me to Christie, one of the girls. I eventually started partying with her when I wasn't out running with Jay.

One night Christie threw a party at her house, and in one of my drunken stupors she came to me.

"Hey, Levi." She kicked my foot as I sat eyes half-open on the couch. "These are my boys, Da'shaun and Jordon. You should kick it with these cats sometime."

Christie had a thing for gangsters, and most of her party guests were thugs. Not just the wannabe kind, but the legit ones, the type that would leave you lying in a dark alley just for looking at them cross-eyed.

Da'shaun and Jordon were raised in the foster-care system, so we had that in common, and despite the fact Da'shaun was black and Jordon was white, they were brothers. Their friends nicknamed them the "Ying Yang brothers," a name swiped from the hip-hop group.

Da'shaun was a big dude, not only tall, but stocky with some meat to spare. When he wasn't rolling with a picked-out Afro, Da'shaun had his locks swept back in tightly braided cornrows. Da'shaun could rap, too, spitting rhymes like a gangster Dr. Seuss. His craft had earned him the proper street cred in the underground urban rap circles of the city.

Jordon was the other half, a tall kid in his midtwenties, with a skinned head and tattoos rolling all along his neck, and every other visible place, for that matter. Most were gang related, and he had so much ink on him it had earned him a dishonorable discharge from the Marines.

We all took to each other the first night we met. There is a silent bond among veterans. You look out for one another. And having endured the foster system gave an added strength to our bond.

They became my closest friends, leaving Jay to find a new taxi driver.

⁓

Da'shaun and Jordon had connections, serious connections, like Mafia ones. Kansas City has an old and established Mafia presence, and the brothers had an in with one of the families. In ways I never stuck my nose into, they had the hookup on some serious weight in drugs. I don't know how they did it, nor did I care, but those two always had a stash of some of the best weed you could ever turn to smoke, the kind that leaves you stupid as you stare at the ceiling contemplating the complexities of life.

Running with Da'shaun and Jordon became my life, and when I wasn't asleep or working at my new serving job at 54th Street Bar and Grill, I was with them, smoking and drinking. For three months straight, there wasn't a moment I was sober. The second I would start to come down, I'd roll another blunt and light up.

I couldn't live life sober, because then the memories would catch up—memories of times long ago, loved ones, and friends lost. So I shut them up with another hit off the blunt or another glass of Jack and Coke.

My boss at 54th didn't care. Da'shaun and Jordon were his hookup, too, so he turned a blind eye and just let me come and go as I pleased.

But it wasn't long until I found a better way to close off my mind from pain inside my soul.

Sex.

Too many beautiful women to count were at the parties Da'shaun, Jordon, and I frequented, and there were plenty who came through the doors of 54th Street. I found a way to use the charm and good looks passed down from my father, and I'd spit some game, get their numbers, and well … you know.

———

A few months into hanging with the brothers, Da'shaun drove me down the block in his tricked-out, old-school Impala, heading to meet the leader of their little gang. Turns out it was his older brother, Darius, a man I had seen briefly once before. He was the type of guy you couldn't meet or get close to without someone vouching for you first and taking you to him.

And there were whispers I had heard about him that are best not repeated. He was a legend to gangsters, and Da'shaun had just parked his lowrider at the curb outside the house.

"Yo, man," Da'shaun said, turning to me, with a voice of reverence, "you got to be cool on this, you feel?"

We stood on the steps, and Da'shaun pushed the walkie on his Nextel. "Yo, bro, we on the porch."

The walkie phone chirped. "A'ight, nigga, get in here," came a deep and hardened voice over the little speaker.

Da'shaun shot me a look: *For real, be cool or you'll be dead, get it?*

"I'm down, man." I tipped my head to Da'shaun. "Let's do this."

"Okay, man, 'cause I like you, and I'd hate to have to ditch your corpse somewhere."

A lump formed in my throat.

We stepped into a darkened house. Thick curtains were drawn in every room, blocking out any means of light and preventing peeping eyes on the street from seeing anyone inside.

Da'shaun turned down the hall and knocked on a bedroom door.

"You good, fool," a voice answered from the other side.

I followed behind Da'shaun, and we stepped into the hazy, smoke-filled bedroom. Darius got up off the waterbed and slipped on a basketball jersey. He was ready to come out of hiding for the day.

"T'is him?" Darius tilted his head toward me, his question aimed at Da'shaun.

"Sho' is, brotha."

"A'ight. Leave us then." Darius eyed me over with the hardened, glassy-eyed look of a killer. Da'shaun tilted a look my way, *hope to see you again, man,* as he left the room.

Darius walked to his dresser and grabbed a pack of Newports off the top. Awkward silence gripped the room as he reached into the top drawer and grabbed something that glinted in the bedroom's twilight. He tucked it in his waistband.

He walked past me and through the door. "Follow me. We's stepping out for a minute."

We crossed though the darkened house and out onto the back deck. Darius leaned against the rail and motioned for me to stand where he could see me. He extended the pack of smokes my way in a peace offering. I lit up along with him, despite the fact I loathed menthol.

"My little brother tells me you's legit." A cloud of carcinogens rolled out of his nostrils. "You's been rolling with them a while now?"

"For some time now, yeah." I took a slow drag off my cigarette.

He paused and stared at me to prove his hardness. "Jordon said something about you were going to be an Army Ranger? That true?"

"Sorta … I was injured the day before selection."

He smiled, as if something I said was pleasing, and his voice drew more sterile. "Then you's not afraid of a fight? Da'Shaun says you threw down on some dudes at a party way back."

"Nah, not really." I leaned back on the deck railing, relaxed now with Darius. "I just don't take it from people—I've had enough of that to last a lifetime."

Darius smirked, took a deep drag, and blew the smoke across the deck. "Can you handle this?" He withdrew a matte black pistol from his waist and put it on the railing in front of me, like a gift.

I eyed the gun, recognizing it as a Glock, a really *nice* Glock. "For sure." I reached out.

He finished his smoke and flicked the butt into the yard.

"You's gonna be running with me now, deal?"

I nodded my head. I was guessing that from the beginning. "You watch my back. Thing is, you snitch or run yo' mouth, and I'll kill you. Feel me?"

My eyes met his. *I got ya, man.*

"A'ight, that's what I thought." He turned his back and motioned for me to follow.

27

EARNING MY STRIPES

I was in—whatever "in" was. Darius had given me an interview of sorts, and I must have lived up to the rep he'd heard about me from the brothers. From that moment on I was in his inner circle, and we were off and running.

The Quindaro, a drug dealer's no-man's land, was his favorite spot. I had been there before, but not like this. Everywhere we went some crackhead on the corner was giving a shout-out to Darius like he ran the avenue.

Darius was a year shy of thirty, ten years older than me, but he'd been in and out of prison during those ten years. He used all the time behind bars to beef up his muscle mass—not that he was small to begin with, standing about six foot four and tipping the scale at an easy 240. Darius had affection for jerseys, slick tennis shoes, and power.

His favorite gun was an all-chrome .357 Magnum that he kept tucked in his waist almost everywhere he went. Darius was hard—*real* hard.

Word was, he was a killer, the kind of man that would snatch the breath out of your body just because he could. And after one look in his eyes, I could vouch to that. He was also the connection to the Italians Da'shaun had boasted about, being that Darius was dating one the families' daughters.

That first run on the Quindaro was the beginning. Over the weeks and months to come, everywhere Darius went, I followed alongside.

A real-life *My Buddy*.

Except with street smarts … and a gun.

I was barely nineteen years old, and I was the right-hand man to a powerful gang leader. One more fatherless kid turned gangbanger. Another statistic.

Right off the bat after meeting Darius, I had to go through a series of initiations to prove my grit. One: a street fight with four guys who heavily outmuscled me. It left me messed up and bloody. In fact, I passed blood-tinted urine for three days after.

Two: I had to break into the house of a mark Darius didn't like, a competitor, and find a stash of cash. The man had run his mouth off to a narc. With that, I proved I was no chump, whatever that meant. I was officially a member of his gang. I had earned my *stripes*. Literally.

Being Darius's protégé was not without benefits. Darius had quite the influence in the little niche of town where my run-down apartment complex was located. Every addict or hustler knew who he was, and they all revered or feared him for the hardness of his soul. I became respected just for my closeness to him.

My apartments were a slum within a slum. Realtors would say they were in need of a little TLC. People who lived outside the area viewed them as a teardown. Most tenants were Section 8 welfare and were either unemployed or addicts. The cops were constantly in and out of the complex or running a patrol down the road that cut through the neighborhood. It was the ghetto.

The crime in that part of town was so bad that cars were broken into in broad daylight, sometimes even stolen—just because. Even when cars all around my ride fell prey to theft and vandalism, mine wasn't touched, a sign I wasn't to be trifled with.

And I drove a nice car, too, funded by plenty of drug money. It was a two-year-old Chevy Impala, painted white pearlescent and rolling on twenty-inch Asanti rims. The trunk rattled with twelve-inch Rockford subwoofers.

A handful of our repeat customers lived in my complex. Even the two maintenance men that worked there came to Darius and me. Knowing who I was and, more importantly, who I knew, the two men kissed up to me, often telling me little whispers they heard in the complex, like which units were under the police's eye, or even passing us the keys of an apartment that might have something Darius and I would like for ourselves.

In the eyes of the residents, Darius and I ran that project. Sometimes the tenants would come to me to help them solve disagreements, like I was some kind of street judge. Even if most of their complaints were petty, that was still kind of cool.

⚊⚊⚊

I was so deep into this lifestyle of violence and thuggery that I received the mark of a legit gang member: a street name. It's a name given as a token of honor and somewhat protects your real identity from someone aiming to rat you out.

Darius's was *Caesar*. He was our undisputed leader, and dating the daughter of a mob boss didn't hurt.

Mine was *Slowdown*.

Da'shaun gave me the name, stemming from times when the brothers would see girls slow down whatever they were doing to check me out. Darius often bragged to the crew that there wasn't a girl I couldn't get.

In those days, there was no denying I was a ladies' man, a player, and a heartbreaker. To the crew, that got me some respect.

And speaking of respect, I earned two "stripes" for busting up some folks in a lick that Darius sent me on with Da'shaun. My internal anger found violence soothing, and I loved fights, even running my mouth to start one.

Darius always wore a Duke Blue Devils cap, which had a likeness of the devil on it. The ugliness of who I had become couldn't be better defined than that symbol on the hat of the man whom I served.

I spent so much time with Darius that I lost all sense of reality, my past, and the man I had once aspired to be. To me that man was long gone, dead along with the dreams he held.

When Darius and I weren't selling a sack of rocks to some addict or pulling a lick on someone who had crossed him, we were off on a getaway. A few times we went down to San Antonio, Texas, and checked into a seedy hotel room where the walls stunk from the guest the night before.

The plan was always the same. We'd meet a pair of Latino gentlemen the next morning in their room and exchange a bag full of cash for some hefty drugs—mostly cocaine and marijuana.

Darius and I were making some serious cash, the kind you don't deposit into your checking account. You either had to find an inventive way of storing it away, or you could always give in to the materialistic temptation of a spending spree. I had everything I wanted, paid in full. Pretty posh for a teenager.

Darius and the brothers had a carnal way of "stimulating the economy." Every so often, Da'shaun would talk one of his "clients" into throwing a party at his house down in the elite part of town—a house big enough to be called a mansion.

Any sinful indulgence you could name, we had it at the party: countless beautiful women, a few exotic dancers, and a buffet of drugs. Business contacts always expanded after one of those events.

And when Darius and I weren't blowing money in Kansas City, we took off via a cheap Southwest flight to Miami or Vegas to hit a strip joint or nightclub.

Running with Darius, the allure of power became the high. For once in my life, I felt as if I had the world in a chokehold. If I wanted something, it became mine. If I didn't like you, you were dealt with.

I felt powerful. I felt respected. I felt untouchable.

But the sad reality was, I was young, dumb, and prideful. Nothing stood testament to that more than one day when I met with my grandpa.

Eleanor had passed away while I was in the army, and Harold left for a prolonged trip to Australia, their favorite vacation spot. When he came back, he gave me a call and was surprised to hear I wasn't in Afghanistan but Kansas City. I was so excited—even in my hardened state—to hear his voice on the other end of the phone. We chose to meet at the Taco Bell not far from his house. He said lunch was on him.

Harold sat across the table and we made small talk, laughing at several life memories. He teased me about finally being able to grow facial hair. But throughout the meal, he had what seemed a wary eye on me. The man was blood and my grandpa, but he wasn't dumb. He also loved me—enough to call me on the carpet.

"Levi," he asked as he took a bite from his soft taco, "where are you getting all this nice stuff?"

I stopped eating, completely taken aback at his question. "You know," I said smiling, trying to throw him off, "just waiting tables at 54th."

His countenance shifted, enough so that even with all his wrinkles, I could see the steel in his expression.

"You mean to tell me you drive that"—he looked to my car sitting outside—"and wear those clothes, by serving food?" His look said, *Don't play me for a fool, Grandson.*

I didn't say anything, but I was annoyed. More at myself than him. How could I ever be mad at him?

"Levi, I saw this with your cousins. You're running with the wrong folks, aren't you?" His eyes welled. "I was so proud of you for going into the army, and I know the accident wasn't your fault. I expect this sort of thing with your cousins. But with you … son, you're better than this. I can't be proud of you for this."

I stared into his eyes and saw the pain that overwhelmed him, and I knew without a doubt that pain had come from my own actions. He might have been old, but he would take it all if he could, if I'd let him. His eyes spoke, *I love you. For me, please don't do this.*

But life had taught me to love only myself.

I stood up from the table, not wanting to face my actions anymore. I reached into my pocket and pulled out a wad of cash, more than enough to cover his meal and mine, and sat it down on the table before him.

"I never asked you to be proud of me," I said in a cold, detached voice, then turned and walked out to my car. I glanced at the window as I was driving away, and I saw him sitting at the table with his head in his hands, shoulders shaking as if crying.

I never took his calls after that, and eventually they ceased.

Two years later, I learned why he had stopped calling with time—he had stopped living. Grandpa Harold passed away one night in his sleep. He'd lived a long and full life, but now he was gone forever. I never got to make our relationship right. I never got to see him proud of me for the *right* reasons.

I never got to tell him one last time, "I love you."

28

"YOU CAN REST WHEN YOU'S DEAD."

Power and respect.

Two facets of life mankind has lusted for since the garden of Eden. I was no different. Yes, I wanted power. I wanted the power to stop this pain that consumed my soul.

However, every attempt I made to fill the ever-deepening anguish only left the void more unsatisfied.

I traveled from one extreme to the next in my search to find anything, anyone who could silence the heartache. Yet in all my foolishness, I never once realized what I longed for was a soul at rest.

But where could I find this peace if not in the arms of a woman, the smoke of a blunt, or the bottom of a cognac bottle?

And ever unsatisfied, I continued my odyssey to find *it!*

~~~

The run was up.

In early September 2003, Darius went back to prison for a parole violation. He had ninety days to think things over—not that it would teach him a lesson. This should have been my wake-up call, but I was born some kind of stubborn, and I just didn't care.

With Darius gone, that left Da'shaun and me as the interim leaders of the crew. Once a week I would head to Darius's house—which actually belonged to his mom—and receive a collect phone call from him, listening carefully as he told me how to take care of business while he was gone.

Since the prison conversations were recorded, he talked in code, telling me how to take care of "his moms" (cocaine) and the "house" (the business). Different rooms in the house—kitchen, hall, bedroom—meant different things or stood for certain people. He may have been locked away, but he was still running the show from inside.

Da'shaun and I found it best to split up. He wasn't really interested in managing things, and while we were still close friends, he just wanted to do his own thing. So I took care of running the organization. Besides, all of Darius's connects knew my face better than Da'shaun's, so I followed through with all the deals.

<hr />

A few days before Christmas, Darius got out of prison. I swung by the downtown Greyhound station and picked him up. Darius didn't want to go home; he wanted to get right back to it and make that money. But first he wanted to see his girl.

I sat on the steps outside her apartment, blowing through my last Black & Mild while he did his thing. The door opened, and he tilted his head toward the car. "Let's roll."

I was driving us across the city to the next deal, acting as his armed chauffeur as usual, when he turned to me.

"Slowdown, I's real proud of you." He rarely smiled as he was now, and when he grinned that big, it meant he was captivated by one of a few things: money, more money, or a hot girl. "You did this legit, watching my ends. For that, yo my nigga fo' life!"

He punched me in the shoulder, his way of a hug.

His "ends" were his drug empire, and I had watched over it with the vigor of an up-and-coming entrepreneur. It had earned his heart, and for some reason his approval of me meant everything.

"Anything you want, man, it's on me. Any day, man, I'll kill fo' you." He was serious. Of course, Darius was *always* serious— unless he was too messed up to put a sentence together, which was often.

<hr />

With Darius there was never a time to rest, his philosophy being, "You can rest when you's dead." Every minute was a chance to make that money.

Money was a god to him. Women were the other idol.

One night he came to me and echoed the words he had said that night in the car.

"Man, I gots a gift fo' yo.'" His smile showed he was as excited for it as I was. "You'll just love it."

The gift turned out to be a girl, not a possession. And while I was no gentleman myself, women to him were simply objects. I could tell by his glee that she was a rare look.

Except with Darius, there were always strings attached.

We went down to the Plaza shopping district, the ritzy part of town, to meet the girl he raved about. The catch: he was going to move a large amount of cocaine through her apartment that weekend, and he wanted me to be the watchdog. I was also free to enjoy the "hospitality" of my hosts.

The girl was Tabitha, and she lived with her mom, Megan. The two were one of the most unique mother-daughter combinations I have ever known, short of watching Jerry Springer.

Tabitha, at nineteen, was a year younger than me now that I'd turned twenty, and her mom didn't look much older since she'd had Tabitha when still in high school.

The two were exemplary proof of what money could buy when it came to enhancing a woman's beauty. Both ladies had received plenty of plastic surgery for this and that, and they were walking Barbie dolls—every man's lustful fantasy. Their quality enhancements had gotten them both in Playboy.

Megan was in her early thirties and lived in a luxury condo off the Plaza. She was an escort, a high-dollar one, the kind that only celebrities, CEOs, and politicians could afford. Her profession often took her across the country. A few days of work a month paid for her and her daughter's extravagant lifestyle.

Tabitha was gorgeous, too, and was groomed to follow in her mother's footsteps. When I first saw her, I fell hard. It wasn't only her flawless beauty, but also because of the look in her eye, the same one I saw every day in my mirror.

It was the look of a soul thrust into a life not of her choosing.

I wanted her, to save her from her own pain—ironic as that was.

For the weekend, I bunkered down at the girls' condo and played the good soldier. Darius returned in a couple days with a few Italian fellows. The entourage moved to the bedroom to transact the business deal.

I lay on the couch with Tabitha in my arms while she slept.

Some movie played on the big screen across the marble floor. My job was officially over, yet I kept one eye on the door that Darius had walked through, ready to do whatever was needed.

An hour later, Darius emerged, his feet stumbling as he walked the two men—who were now carrying a large piece of Louis Vuitton luggage—out of the condo. When Darius returned from the lobby, he locked the front door, popped off the lights in the unit, and disappeared into the bedroom with Megan.

I flicked off the TV as Tabitha nestled into my arms and smiled. Having done my duty for the day, I closed my eyes and went to sleep.

"Slowwwwdooowwnn!" Darius's voiced bellowed through the condo.

I bolted up off the couch, dumping Tabitha on the floor.

What was that? I had never heard his voice like that before. I rushed toward the bedroom, shooting a glance around the place, checking the locks to make sure we were alone.

I threw open the door and swept the room with my glance. Darius was standing at the foot of the bed, sweat dripping down his forehead. I was also staring down the barrel of his .357.

"You's a —— cop, man?" he swore, and spit shot from his mouth and formed scum in the corners. His eyes darted around the room like a spooked cat, and his pupils were dilated. His whole body twitched in little movements, but the gun never wavered much.

"Be easy, man." I lifted my hands palm out, showing my peaceful intention. "Man, you know I'm no cop!"

Megan was passed out under the sheets. Several empty travel-size bottles of alcohol were strewn across the floor, and a small mountain of cocaine sat on a round vanity mirror beside the bed. Even though you should never mix the two, I knew both were surging through

Darius's bloodstream. He'd done that particular cocktail before but had never acted this paranoid.

"Dar, you need to eat something, bro." I took a half step forward, showing him I was safe. "Put down the piece, and let's go to the Waffle House, man. On me."

He swore at me again, the gun rattling in his hand, shaking from his desire to pull the trigger. "'ou's a——cop!"

"Man … I'm no cop." I tried to smile. "Trust me!"

"A'ight … snort that!" He tilted his head to the pile of cocaine behind him. "'Cause if you's a cop, you won't do it!"

There was no way I could do what he was asking, even if I'd wanted to. While cocaine had never been my thing, the amount he was asking me to ingest would have killed me a hundred times over.

"Man, be easy. You know I can't do that much."

"'Cause you a cop!" he growled. The hatred in his voice could have shaken the pits of hell.

The words were barely out of his mouth when he closed the short distance between us and slammed the pistol into the side of my head. My vision blurred and dimmed, and I collapsed to the floor.

I sprawled, dazed. When I tried to stand, he put his foot on my chest and stomped me to the ground, then kicked me in the head with his other foot. I lay there semiconscious as he repeatedly kicked my head and chest, cursing, and waving that chrome pistol. I knew he was going to kill me, and my hand instinctively slid into my waistband and wrapped around the Glock he'd given me a year earlier. I was going to kill him first. His kicks made it hard to concentrate as I struggled to get the gun free.

Tabitha rushed into the room. "Stop it, Darius!" Her voice was still hoarse with sleep. She pushed against Darius, a man twice her size. "Stop it! Get off him!"

Darius stopped and took a step backward as if he had snapped back to reality. The Glock was still under my belt. I relaxed my grip on it as I watched him wipe at the sweat pouring off his face, relieved he'd come to his senses.

He looked at Tabitha and, with one hand, threw her hard to the ground. In the same motion, Darius twisted his fingers into the hair on the back of my head and shoved his knee into my abdomen, using the full weight of his body to bury the Glock. He'd seen me going for it. His revolver pressed hard into the cheekbone below my eye. I smelled the brass bullets inside, and I looked into the deep reservoir of malice and rage in his eyes. His right eye twitched. He was going to do it.

Without a word, he lifted me by the neck, dragged me into the hallway outside the condo, and threw me down, his gun still pointed at my face.

"I ever see you again"—he seemed sober now—"I'll——kill you!"

He disappeared behind the closed door, and I heard the deadbolt drop. I leaned my head back and took a breath of relief, my brain still foggy from the blows. As quickly as I could manage, I got up and fled before Darius returned with his threat.

The entire short walk to the elevator, I never took my eyes off the condo door. I had finally gotten the Glock out, but my whole arm trembled as I held the gun against my leg.

It was early morning, and no one stirred in the building. Then again, these were luxury apartments with thick walls.

Ding. The elevator arrived and the doors opened. I immediately stepped inside and repeatedly hit the command button to close the door.

Slow to respond, the doors lazily came together, sealing me away from the hallway and the condo. Inside the muffled bunker, I slid down the wall into a relieved lump and took a deep breath.

And just like that, I was gone. As the elevator descended, it was if each floor stripped away another layer: power, respect, money, privilege, membership in the inner circle.

29

THE QUESTION

Adrenaline kept me coherent long enough to get out of harm's way, but it was fast flushing from my battered system. I held it together just long enough to exit the building and drive a few blocks away to a grocery store parking lot, where under the protective anonymity of an outlying light pole, I reclined my car seat and gave in to a physical blackout.

~~~

By the time I made it back to my place, pain was pulsing through my entire chest. I stumbled through the front door and leaned against the wall. I couldn't get air, and each breath sent a sharp stitch into my lungs. It was like I'd been run over by a car.

I walked to the fridge, grabbed the chilled bottle of Hennessy cognac, and downed a handful of swigs—enough to curb the pain and put me into a deep sleep.

Hours later, I woke to searing chest pain. Sleep hadn't helped, and even my heart beating caused me to break out in sweat. Somehow, I slid out of bed and hobbled down to my car. I needed help.

I made my way to the ER, where a nurse asked me a lot of questions and promptly led me to an exam room. A few tests and several hundred dollars later, I found out I had two cracked ribs. Several more were bruised.

The doctor gave me a script for oxycodone, a narcotic I was well familiar with. I filled it at the hospital, then disappeared back to the protective warmth of my bed, while daylight filtered through the shades drawn over the window.

I laid low for the next two weeks, not even bothering with 54th Street. Doctor's orders, after all. It was a good excuse because I didn't want to run into Darius anytime soon. He had called a few times, leaving no message.

＝〜〜〜＝

For some time, I had a "friend" living with me in the other room of my two-bedroom apartment. Her name was Shae, and she was the one girl who stayed constant. All the other girls I brought into my life changed whenever I felt so inclined. Shae was a friend and a coping mechanism that helped me keep my mind from wandering to the painful places I didn't want it to go.

Shae was tall, with long black hair that draped to her waist, and graced with the perfect skin of a china doll along with ice-blue eyes that lit the windows to her soul. I had met her through Da'shaun and Jordon at a party one night, and we became close after that.

She had grown up a California girl but left home when her father became abusive. Shae ended up going to college at KU for a law degree, specializing in criminal justice. That's irony for you. I was probably the subject of some of her papers.

Shae was every man's heartthrob: attractive, smart, nurturing, and incredibly ambitious. I never let myself see her for who she really was—until it was too late. I was too busy being a narcissist, living life by my own terms, and using her for my own selfish gains.

Despite that I grossly took her for granted, Shae had always stuck by my side. And now that I was banged up, she looked out for me yet again while I recovered.

With hours of nothing to do but stare at my bedroom ceiling, my mind began to drift to the places I had fought so hard to forget. I was forced the hard way to come to terms with my own physical addictions: I ran out of pain pills sooner than I should have, and my personal stash of drugs was long gone. All the people I was busy avoiding were my sources for all things narcotic.

＝〜〜〜＝

One drugless night, I lay on my bed in too much pain to sleep. The ceiling fan twirled above me in a hypnotic dance. When I concentrated, I could count its slow rotations. I closed my eyes one more time, hoping the next time I'd open them would be the dawn of a new day.

"When will you ever change?" the voice of a man came from somewhere in my room.

My eyes bolted open, and I sat up slowly and looked around.

Did I just hear someone say—

"When will you ever change?" the voice repeated, this time resonating through my soul.

I had heard it clearly. Chills scurried along my spine while goose bumps rippled my arms. Instinct was to reach for my gun, but something told me that while I should be afraid, no weapon could save me from this.

Was this ... God?

I had heard this voice before as a young boy in the darkened bedroom of my uncle's house. *This can't be happening. I was a boy then, and scared ... but now ...*

I shifted out of my bed and walked to Shae's room, easing open the door.

"*Pssst!* ... Shae ... did you ..." I whispered, as if to hide from the voice.

"Levi," Shae interrupted, her face buried under her pillow. I leaned closer to make out her sleep-blurred words. "You guys gotta keep it down! I've got a test first thing in the morning." She let out a sigh and went back to sleep.

I gulped. *You guys? She'd heard it, too!* I slipped back into my room and sat on the edge of the bed, contemplating what in the world was going on. *Am I losing my mind, or what?*

"When will you ever change?" the voice came a third time, softly now, sounding as if he were sitting next to me on the bed.

I began to sweat as my eyes blurred with tears. I took a deep, slow breath. My ribs creaked, and I winced with pain. This was no narcotic wearing off, nor a symptom of withdrawal from my addictions.

It was God—and he had a question for me.

30

THROWING IN
THE TOWEL

I f you were able to ask God one question, what would you ask? What
if he was to ask *you* one question?

"When will you ever change?"

Frankly, I hadn't expected *any* questions from God. My plan for
him was to intervene on my behalf, change *things* around me. But *me*
change? Did God really just ask me that? Yes, he did.

I could continue to run, but right then I realized I could no longer hide. Everything I thought I knew flipped upside down as his one
question turned my world right side up.

〰

I thought I'd seen a few things in my days on earth, but this
trumped all. Even if I wanted to ignore the question, I couldn't get the
sound of his voice out of my head. It was a voice broken with love, love
for someone who had pushed him away.

If the heartbreak wasn't sufficient by itself, the authority behind
his voice was enough to shake my soul with fear—more commanding
than all the thugs, cops, and soldiers I had ever met.

But how could the Creator of all that existed be heartbroken
over *me*?

〰

I leaned back on my bed and sat there wide awake. For hours I
mulled this over as the sun crept over the horizon and its light fell
gently across the foot of my bed. My soul was haunted by his question.

Just what, exactly, did I need to change?

I never said a word about the voice to anyone over the next few days. Each day was a rerun of the previous except for the uneasy rot that grew in the depth of my gut. For the first time in a long while, I began feeling remorse.

A few days later, Jennifer, a friend of mine who I'd been seeing on the side, invited me to see the movie *The Passion of The Christ*. It was irony at its finest and maybe even God's design to finally get through to me.

Jennifer and I sat in the darkened theater and watched the story of Jesus, whose pictures I had taken off my walls as a child because they'd given me the creeps. I'd done my best to forget about him. Yet, oddly, he was the one I would call on if I ever felt inclined to pray.

My mind reeled throughout the movie—the voice, the question—and I struggled to concentrate on the film. *Change … change … change? What's wrong with me that I need to change?* Over and over this question needled my sanity.

What if everything we thought about God is wrong? Chaplain Wes's question popped into my head as I watched the flickering images of Jesus being nailed to the cross.

The man on the next cross—a man just like me, a thug, a criminal—spoke to Jesus. "Lord, when you enter your kingdom, remember me." A tear slid down the convict's cheek, sorrow for the life he had lived.

Then the God-Man, suffocating by his own execution, pushed to lift himself up on the tree where he was nailed, gasped a lungful of air, enough to utter words that would change the criminal's life. "Today, you will be with me in paradise." Christ's eyes met those of the convict, who bowed his head in thanks.

And there was only love in his gaze.

Love. I now realized I had never really known it.

Not because no one had ever offered. There had been plenty: my mother, Grandpa Harold, Mr. Redding, Ms. Boyden, Naomi, Parker, the Rosettas. But I had pushed them all away so love couldn't take root, same as I'd done to the man who was dying on the screen before my eyes.

Love—my resistance had transformed me into a soulless man.

When the Christ spoke those onscreen words to a man who might have well been me, it became clear what the voice in my bedroom wanted. I needed to stop pushing love away; stop pushing *him* away.

I stood from my seat, and Jennifer shot me a glance as if to say, *Wait, where are you going? You're missing the whole point of this movie.*

No, I got the point of the movie.

"I'll be back," I choked, fighting back sobs that were threatening to disrupt the whole theater. Half-blind, I stumbled down the steps and into the restroom off the lobby. My forehead beaded with sweat, and I shoved open a stall door with a trembling palm. Locked inside, I flushed the toilet over and over as I leaned against the wall and cried.

"I get it … I get it … I need to change," I whispered between sobs.

I stepped out of the stall and splashed water on my face at the grimy sink. The eyes staring back at me in the mirror revealed a weathered soul, a boy forced to be a man too soon, a man who had pushed everyone away to feel nothing anymore. Words from those in my past, those who had loved me, swirled in my mind. I was sorry for those I'd hurt, who I'd become.

I needed a change. No, I needed *to* change.

And I wanted what I had just seen in the film. I wanted love.

I had barely snuck back to the theater entry when the credits began to roll. Jennifer was sitting in her seat, awaiting my return. She met me, and we merged with the solemn crowd.

"You all right?" she asked as we walked to the car.

"I'm good." I shot her a façade-laden smile. "Just needed to hit the restroom."

A storm was rolling in, and thunder echoed in the distance as raindrops began falling around us. Thankfully, the rain and our sprint to the car broke Jennifer's fixation on my disappearance.

I dodged with the best. "You hungry?"

She smiled, and I took that as a *yes*. I detoured to the drive-thru at Taco Bell on the way back to my place. Jennifer tried to make small talk about the downpour rattling the tin roof of my Chevy, but my mind was scrolling through the places I'd walked in my life.

We hurried into my apartment, shaking water off our clothes. Jennifer flicked on the light while I took our food to the kitchen table. I stopped and looked around. Something was off. For a moment, I wondered if Darius was inside somewhere. I hadn't taken my gun with me.

But then I saw the note lying on the stove. Gorgeous cursive strokes penned my name.

Levi

I tore it open.

I loved you—and you never cared.

I ran to Shae's room. The closet was open and empty. A mark in the dust was all that showed where her clock radio had once perched on the nightstand.

I sagged against the wall.

Shae was gone. All that lingered was the faint smell of her Chanel perfume.

I was beginning to realize all the people I had walked on, all those who had loved *me,* and I had never cared. Even though Shae had been the one to leave, I'd been the one to walk out on her. Then there was God.

God had loved me, and I had never cared.

His hand might as well have penned that note, just as I knew he'd hung the Footprints poem in my foster parents' house.

Boom! Lightning struck close by, and its wake of thunder shook the building. Jennifer shrieked in surprise. For me, it only sent my thoughts deeper toward God, to what a wise man had said to me.

Go to the center of the storm … God wants to meet you there, to prove he is love.

My hands shook, the notepaper trembling as I read Shae's words one more time. Jennifer came to me, peering into my face and noticing the teardrops stuck to my eyelashes. She rubbed them away with her thumb.

"Levi, are you…"

I pushed past her, out through my apartment door. I was into the storm before I registered her "…okay?"

In the brief sprint to my car, the rain drenched me, washing away the hot tears that soaked my cheeks. I had my car in reverse and was peeling out of the parking lot before I could even think.

The Chevy surged past the speed limit as I took the freeway onramp. I didn't have a clue as to my destination. I just drove and drove as my windshield wipers fought with the torrents of rain that streamed across the glass.

So many times, God's words of love had coursed into my life, some through the hand or words of others, some in unexplainably miraculous ways.

"God will only be a stranger to you if you let him … Only you can let him in … He's not like other men … I love you with a love beyond your understanding. I have always loved you, and I will never stop loving you … Wherever you go, I will always be with you, by your side, no matter what … The years when you have seen only one set of footprints, my child, is when I carried you … Go to the eye of the storm. God wants to meet you there, and prove to you he is love … I loved you, and you never cared."

I can't explain the feeling when my soul tore open and lay bare to the reality that I am loved. New tears of sorrow for pushing God's love away streamed down, adding to the watery view of the road.

Beyond the rain rolling over my windshield, I spotted a park along the river. I jerked the wheel for the exit and made my way down a couple of streets. Lightning forked across the sky, impossibly shaking even more water from the twisting clouds. I slammed on the brakes, straddling two parking places. Mine was the only vehicle in sight. I swung the door open, and a cascading waterfall blew in. I got out and closed the door to protect the interior. But there was no protection for me as I walked toward the river. A bench sat facing the other shore, somewhere beyond the storm, and I slogged to it.

⸻

I dropped my head into my hands as I wept while the early spring rain splattered on around me. A bolt of lightning pierced the night sky, and I tensed, waiting for the thunder.

Ka-booommm! The explosion vibrated the soggy ground beneath my tennis shoes.

The noise shook me loose from my thoughts and back to my current reality. I looked toward the sky, to the One I wanted to see. At least this is what I tried to do; the increasing downpour ran into my eyes and made it impossible. I struggled to form words as I squinted into the expanse above.

"God ... why?" I yelled into the heavens, with a voice as tight as a clenched fist. "Why? Why did you let this ... any of this ... happen in my life?"

No longer could I run from this question, as it was the one question I would ask of God if given the chance. *Why?*

Rain merged with the tears that flowed from the unrelenting pain of life. *My life*, and all I had known.

And why *this* particular park? This was where the Missouri River separated Missouri and Kansas. Just a few yards away it seethed and churned with the heavy rains, threatening to overrun its banks. It was scary, threatening, magnificent.

Maybe my subconscious had guided me here, or maybe someone wanted me to be here at a place where nature was on the verge of losing its peaceful tranquility to an all-consuming, destructive force that would swallow anything in its path. Ironically, this is how it was with the emotions that lay beneath the waters of my heart—generally peaceful on the outside, but only moments from a relentless fury of anguish.

All I knew was that in this moment my heart and soul were crying out. I wanted the pain to stop.

God ... you have to hear me! I can't do this anymore ... I just ... can't.

Would he help, though? Would the One who created the heavens and earth—who could have stopped the wreck of my life, my pain, before it ever happened—would he really listen and prove he was there? Would he really hear ... me?

After all, how did I get to this point in life? I mean, my life had been messed up practically from the moment I was born. How could I stop it?

I was a soul tormented by life, and I was alone in the rain. It didn't have to be the middle of the night for me to feel all alone. That's how I always felt. *Alone.*

One last time I looked to the sky, to the One who could end it all and prove to me that he cared. No, more than that ... that he loved *me*!

There was only one thing I could think of to fix this. I stood from the soggy bench that had been my exposed refuge this night and walked the dozen steps to the river's edge. With the sky thundering above and the river raging inches before me, there was only one thing left I could do.

A lump of uncertainty blocked my throat. My next action ... well, there would be no turning back. I leaned back to fully confront the storm's fury, and with effort, cleared my throat. With one last glance to the river, I pursed my lips and lifted my eyes toward heaven so I could speak to God.

"I ... I give up!"

And with that, I closed my eyes and flung myself forward onto my knees.

"God ... I can't do this anymore. I need a change. I need love. I need you!"

I leaned back, taking in the fury of the storm as rain poured down around me.

"*I need you!*" I shouted into the heavens.

It was time to *change*. It was time for *love*. It was time for *God!*

31

HOUSECLEANING

R edemption.
An existence where the hand of God *rewrites* all that was once wrong!

For this weary soul, it had been a long time coming. In all the delay, God was enduringly patient beyond all comprehension.

While some call his forbearance "long-suffering," I know it only as one thing—*love!*

And his love was about to rewrite all I had ever known.

———

I remained in the park most of the night, alone except for memories of moments past. At some point, the thunderstorm had moved on, and it now echoed far in the distance, lightning still flickering on the horizon.

Clouds billowed overhead, fractured now as moonlight filtered down onto the rushing river. The smell of rain, clean and fresh, hung in the air, and I breathed deeply. My gaze went to the sky.

Go to the eye of the storm. God wants to meet you there, in this, and prove to you he is love. A smile broke over my face at the thought of wise words spoken over me years earlier by a man who had walked my same road.

———

Exhausted and soaked to the bone, I climbed the stairs to my third-floor apartment, my shoes sloshing every step. I flicked on the light as I stepped inside.

Uh oh. Jennifer bolted up from a nap on the couch. Black streaks from the day's mascara stained her cheeks. I had completely forgotten she was here.

"Are you okay, Levi?" She began to cry again. "You can't just leave like that. I thought something might have happened to you!"

I scoffed inwardly at my own selfishness. Yet again someone had cared, and again I walked out on them.

"I'm okay. It's just been a long night."

"What were you doing?" She took a tissue from her purse and wiped her face. "You just took off."

"I was"—I took a breath, preparing myself for what I was about to say—"talking to God."

The look on her face, followed by the silence in the room, was priceless, and I almost smiled.

"You were *what?*" Her eyes narrowed, and her whole face contorted as if she wasn't sure she'd heard me right.

"I was talking to God." I spoke a little louder, sort of amazed at my confidence in that statement.

Jennifer stared at me, bewildered at what I had just admitted.

"Look, it's late." I grabbed her coat and purse and motioned to the door. "I'll walk you out to your car."

A couple minutes later, she smiled and waved as she pulled away, and then I made for my room, dry PJs, and a warm bed. My eyelids were just closing as the dawn of a new day shone across the sky, the storm a thing of distant memory.

⌁⌁⌁

I slept only a few hours before the sunlight beaming on my face woke me up. I blinked and rolled carefully out of bed, my ribcage still tender from Darius's whooping two weeks ago.

As I stood at the sink brushing my teeth, I looked into the mirror, and for the first time I saw a man who was no longer on the run. The past was inexplicably gone, and I looked into a soul at peace. It was almost as if life had been born again.

I must be losing it!

I splashed hot water on my face before heading to the kitchen for breakfast, or what really should have been lunch. It was when I opened the fridge that I realized I was *really* losing it.

Every day for two years, I woke up and poured a glass of alcohol-laden Kool-Aid, my breakfast "juice," while I smoked the day's first cigarette. But today, the sight of the Apple Pucker schnapps made my stomach nauseous. I sat in a kitchen chair in front of the open refrigerator, staring at that bottle and the bottle of Hennessy next to it, and zoned out—my brain not able to grasp what was going on.

Huh ... that's weird.

Without conscious thought, I brought the trash can over to the fridge and scooped all the bottles of alcohol off the top shelf, sending them crashing into the plastic waste bin. It just seemed like the right thing to do.

I took one step toward the door to carry the load down to the Dumpster when I stopped midstep and glanced at the freezer compartment. Although I hadn't opened it, my eyes seemed to see through the steel door of the Maytag. When I opened the door, a carton of Marlboros stared me down. I snatched it—and then gathered the few loose packs laying around my apartment—and tossed them into the trash can as well. A new home awaited them in the bottom of the Dumpster outside.

Back inside, I noticed my cell phone was lit up with several missed calls and text messages. Jennifer had been responsible for most of them, though one was from Darius, apologizing for, in his words, "a bad trip." Dude was more than trippin' all right. He'd put a gun to my head and told me he'd kill me. But things with him were never that straightforward. His apology was more likely because he needed me to watch his back. I had been his right hand and had vastly grown his empire in our days together. Without me, he would be back to dealing and watching his own back. The apology sure wasn't out of sincere remorse.

I shook my head in disgust and snapped my phone closed.

My eyes turned to the world beyond my living room window. A flock of birds strutted on the courtyard below, pecking at bugs in the grass.

My thoughts began to wander. The walls of my apartment seemed to press in, suffocating me. I needed some fresh air. I grabbed my keys and left my apartment; I crossed the parking lot and just kept going.

I let my feet take me where they wanted to go, and that turned out to be several miles down twisting roads and through neighborhoods as I walked for hours. And when I was back inside my place, I crashed on the sofa for a nap, my calves radiating with pain.

When I woke for the second time that day, I saw my phone was lit up again with missed alerts from the usual suspects: three missed calls from Jennifer, a text from Darius, and a voicemail from … Jennifer's parents?

What are they doing calling me? They didn't even know me.

Jennifer's parents were heavy churchgoing folks. They had heard from their daughter about last night's events. They wanted to help—with an offer to get away with them for a week at their upcoming family reunion in Oklahoma. A getaway was exactly what I needed, a chance to clear my mind.

They were leaving early the next morning. Whatever it was that prompted them to invite a kid they didn't know—a drug dealer at that—was beyond me. They did, though, and I wasn't going to second-guess as to why. I needed that time away to think and plan.

It turned out to be kind of a strange trip for me. We spent the time doing normal things: cookouts at people's homes, going out to dinner, sitting around and listening to stories. It was surreal, so far removed from what I'd been used to that I could barely relate, but I had a good time.

The night after returning from Oklahoma, Jennifer, her sister Lauren, and I were sitting in my car at a stoplight. We had just been at the Cheesecake Factory for a late lunch. Rush-hour traffic was at a standstill on eastbound I-70, and I'd exited onto surface streets in what proved a futile plan of a faster route to their house.

As I waited for the red light to change, I heard the voice again.

I love you with a love greater than anything you can know; it's what you have always longed for!

Goose bumps rippled along my arms. I gulped down a lump in my throat, and I glanced nonchalantly at the girls. Jennifer was turned in the passenger seat and immersed in conversation with her sister, who sat in back.

"Please, tell me"—I noticed Jennifer turn at my interruption—"tell me you heard that!"

"Heard what?" Jennifer, annoyed that I'd interrupted with such a dumb question, rolled her eyes and went back to talking to Lauren like nothing had happened.

I'm really losing it. This almost doesn't seem … real. And then he spoke again.

If you leave it all behind—everything—and come to me, I will reveal this love to you in undeniable ways!

I gripped the steering wheel so hard my knuckles turned white, a vain attempt to keep my eyes from tearing up. I had almost reassured myself that I was okay, when …

Will you leave it all behind and follow me, so I can prove my love, prove how unstoppable it is for you?

A single tear slid down my cheek.

Honk! Annoyed horns blared behind me, snapping me back to the moment. Cars in the other lane rushed past on the green light.

Jennifer nudged my arm as I put my foot to the gas. "Levi, you okay?"

I cleared my throat. "Umm, yeah. I just had something in my throat." But it still didn't go away.

The girls had gone inside, but I sat and stared through my windshield at the flowers blooming by their front porch.

What is happening to me?

God had just spoken to me … as if we were friends riding in the car together.

What does a man do with that?

I fiddled with my car keys, chest shuddering with emotion. He'd only asked questions, and I was left to offer answers. Words are inadequate in times like these. My answers would have to be action.

Jennifer came out of her folks' house after some time and leaned her upper body through my window.

"Hey, you. Wanna come inside?"

I sat silent for a moment, seeing her but still focused on something I couldn't see. "Sorry, I have to go take care of something."

Uncertain of what I meant, Jennifer shrugged her shoulders, "O-kay ... umm, well you can come in when you get back, I guess?"

I gave her a warm smile with a nod, put my car in reverse, and backed down the cobblestone driveway and onto the road.

I knew what I was going to do. Besides, what did I have to lose?

32

OFF THE GRID

The sun had become a red ball flattened on its bottom, and I watched it slip below the horizon while I slowly drove around my neighborhood. When it was nearly full dark, I snuck into my apartment.

I couldn't let anyone see me. Too many people knew who I was, what I had been, and if they started asking questions, we were going to have a problem. What would I say, "Sorry, y'all, I don't want to play gangsta no more"?

Yeah, that'd work. That'd just get me shot up with my body ditched behind the strip club in North town. People in my neighborhood like to run their mouths to anyone who will listen—all the way to Darius.

I had come back to do one thing: leave it all behind and follow after *love*.

I flew through my apartment, closed the blinds, and grabbed everything … and I mean everything. In a few short hours, I had the place entirely cleaned out. Only my clothes and the stuff I absolutely had to take went in my car.

A few people had gathered at the Dumpster where I had tossed away all the rest of my belongings: flat-screen television, clothes I didn't want, colognes, and every other furnishing I had in my place. The Dumpster was already half-full when I began, but now it was over-flowing with my stuff. Because they wouldn't fit inside, I had stacked a sofa set, tables, chairs, and a bed alongside the bin. People shamelessly scavenged my unwanted belongings.

I kept my head down as much as possible, but one person stopped to ask, "What are you doin', man?"

He was a crackhead I had sold to frequently. I reached in my pockets and pulled out a wad of cash.

"Here." I made sure he caught my seriousness before I gave it to him. "You saw nothin'. Got it?"

"Yeah, Slowdown," he said, his eyes lighting up as I handed him a hundred bucks. "Whatever you say, man." He gave me a decayed-tooth smile.

Before I could finish the exodus, I had two stops to make. First, I dodged into the main office with my apartment keys and a handwritten letter that read: "I'm ending my lease effective today. Sorry for the troubles."

A thousand dollars filled the envelope. A lick and a drop into the after-hours box, and I was out of there.

One thing remained before I could drop off the face of the earth and permanently cut ties to my past.

Stars shone down as moonlight glinted on the river. These peaceful waters had been a violent torrent the last time we were together. The smell of mud and water filled the night, along with the Acqua di Gio cologne wafting off my shirt.

I lowered my head and closed my eyes in reverence to the moment. *All for love and the One who spoke to me.*

The river gurgled. I opened my eyes, turned to my tricked-out, pearl-white Chevy, and popped the trunk.

A few things remained, things I couldn't throw in the Dumpster, things that couldn't come with me where I was going. Besides, I no longer wanted or needed them.

The first trip to the river, I sent a large bag stuffed with three pounds of royal-blue-colored marijuana to the bottom of the Missouri. I'd weighted it down with rocks, and laughed at the thought of a catfish eating the ripped Smurf Grass. He'd be paranoid for the rest of his life.

Then I went back to the car and removed the towel covering a laundry basket in my trunk. Several matte black guns shone dully in the dim light of my taillights. I scooped them up and, bracing myself on the raised bank, heaved the cache into the water. They splashed and plopped, and in seconds the flow evened out so there was no hint of what had just gone under. But I wasn't done.

As I looked to the sky and smiled at the moon in the cloudless night, I reached underneath my shirt and into my waistband, curled my fingers around the Glock, and brought the pistol into the light.

It was the very gun Darius had given me to watch his back; a gun I would have used to kill him had I needed to; and the symbol of who I had become the past two years.

I stood there for a moment, remembering all the places we'd been in the days prior. As if releasing myself from my old life, I dropped the clip of .40 caliber rounds and worked the slide to eject the one in the chamber. With a mighty windup, I flung the piece, the magazine, and the single bullet as far as I could into the river.

I realized this was the first time in my life that I had truly surrendered. It's not that I didn't have any more fight left in me, but the thing was, I didn't want to fight God anymore.

There was one more thing to ditch, and I was halfway from my car to the river and about to let it fly when I stopped. The Ziploc bag in my hand was full of rubber-banded hundreds—an easy twelve thousand dollars. Drug money. Money that would eat a hole in my conscience if I kept it. But, as I stared at the peaceful river sliding by, I thought, *Why don't I give it to that guy I heard was coming to town?*

I backed away from the river, made sure no one saw me, and slipped the bag of bills back into my car underneath the clothes piled in my backseat.

Finished with my tasks, I made my way to the other side of Kansas City, far from all who had known my face, my name, and my reputation. In a few hours that early April evening, I turned my back on all I had known.

I'd done it for one thing: love.

And I didn't stop driving until I reached a place where no one would come looking.

33

NO TURNING BACK

There's no turning back.

Not that I wanted to, but I sure couldn't turn back now. I was in *this* for good, no matter what. The One who calls himself God had spoken to me and made an offer I couldn't refuse.

Leave it all behind, follow me, and you will find what you have always longed for. Love.

So I did.

I left it all behind. The drugs. The money. The power. And the girls. What had once been my entire existence was no longer reality. Now was the hour for one man's redemption.

⁓⁓⁓

I had escaped to the opposite corner of Kansas City, where I'd found an out-of-the-way motel to stay for the night. My bones ached with weariness, and the pillow on the bed beckoned. Before lying down, I made sure the "Do Not Disturb" sign was hung on the other side of the door. The sun would be up soon, and I didn't want housekeeping rapping on the door in a couple of hours.

When I awoke, I made my way down to the Pakistani gentleman behind the counter to buy a week's worth of sleep time at his Motel 6.

I had exactly one week to make some money the legit way, or I would be out on the street. I'd been a street veteran in earlier years and didn't care to repeat the experience.

Though I had a job at 54th Street Grill, I wasn't going back.

People would come looking for me there, and I didn't want to be found. But before I could go out job searching, I needed a new image.

I swung by a Walgreens down the road and bought a package of razors, a pair of scissors, and some hair dye. The poor motel maid had a mess on her hands when I finished in the bathroom. Hair lay strewn across the floor, and what I hadn't cut off with the scissors was now dyed black, a far cry from the bleach-tipped spikes I previously favored. The goatee was history, too, my chin now clean shaven like my army days.

If I didn't recognize the man in the mirror, the folks who might come looking wouldn't recognize me either.

A Tires Plus down the road got the better end of a deal, too. I rolled up with my tricked-out Chevy with a barter deal. "You can have the rims and sound system if you swap them out for stock and take the tint off my windows."

The kid across the counter, Marcus, stared at me as if I was stupid. "So … you want me to *un*customize your ride?"

I smiled. "Right on, man."

The store manager was ecstatic to take all the kit off my hands, and in a few hours my car looked like a stock sedan, not a drug dealer's whip.

The next day I walked along a sidewalk in downtown Kansas City, scanning the building address numbers. Finally, I found the right doorway.

I hadn't heard of this man before my week with Jennifer's family at the reunion, but they'd talked about him and his coming visit constantly. A man on some kind of crusade. A man they revered as someone who knew God. Jennifer's parents were volunteers at his campaign headquarters, and Jennifer's text with the address was spot on.

The aroma of Folgers coffee from the plant a few blocks upwind tingled my nostrils as I wrestled the spring breeze for entry through the plate-glass door. The noise of the bustling traffic on Main Street muffled quickly as the door swung closed behind me. Except for phones buzzing behind a warren of low cubicles, the office was quiet.

"Sir, can I help you?" A small, middle-aged woman with an obviously overkilled perm stood from behind the reception desk.

"I think so." I looked her over, as I glanced around the room to see who, if anyone, might be watching. "I have something for Mr. Billy Graham."

"Oh." Her face squinted, obviously wondering why a semi-punk kid would be asking for Reverend Graham. "Well, I'm sorry, but he isn't here at this time. He won't actually be here until the crusade begins. Is there something I can do for you?"

Her words were polite, but I had the feeling she was a bit suspicious, especially when I shrugged the backpack off my shoulder, unzipped it, and reached inside.

"Could you please make sure he gets this?" I pulled out the large Ziploc and laid it on her desk. The woman's face grew pale, and she gasped.

"Uhhh…" Her eyes ping-ponged between the bag of money and me, and she gave her head a little shake. "What is it you want me … to … um, do with this?"

"Like I said"—I smiled, trying to hold back an outburst of laughter—"I want to give this to Billy Graham."

The lady's hands trembled as she plopped into her chair and fumbled inside the bottom desk drawer. Her voice disappeared into the cabinet. "Okay … let me … now where? … Ah, there it is."

Her head came back up and she waved a bound pad of paper at me. "I've got your tax donation receipt." She picked up a pen and poised above the pad. "I just need your name and address—"

My heart skipped. I interrupted her by placing my hand on hers. "That won't be necessary." Our eyes met, and I tried to be assertive, but not intimidating. "I just want to give this to you … for Mr. Graham. Please, let's just leave it at that."

"Okay?" She blinked, sounding unsure, like she didn't grasp what I was doing.

I took a few steps back and, without saying a word, made my way through the exit as her voice trailed behind. "But sir … this is tax deductible!"

What didn't she get? It's not like I planned on reporting this on my taxes! I tried not to run as I made my way down the block toward my car.

The farther I got from that bag of money, the more my gait slowed. My nervousness transformed to lightness, to joy. I realized this was the last of it. *All of it.*

There was nothing left of my old life. All was new ... and I was no longer a rubberband man.

I smiled as I looked up at the skyline of clouds and sun-reflecting skyscrapers. My mouth formed silent words to the One above.

Thank you.

And now it was time to embark on my journey to find love, once and for all.

EPILOGUE

Epilogues are supposed to wrap things up and include a little bit of wisdom from the author about what he or she just wrote. I can't give you that. I just have some street smarts and stubbornness. And I am still on the journey myself. So all I can do is be real.

What I can tell you is this: Life will fail you. People will fail you—even those you love, those you count as friends, those you trust. But God won't. That's the takeaway I can leave with you. To trust the struggle, trust Him in it and with it. And remain steadfast that God is stronger than all others, even when it doesn't seem like it or make sense, and especially when you want to give up the most. Life will always be a struggle until the day we breathe our last breath.

Trust your struggle.

I know that it has been God, *and a whole lot of grace*, that has gotten me through to this day. I echo the words of the apostle Paul, "But by the grace of God I am what I am, and his grace to me was not without effect." I've grown up a lot in the decade plus since I stepped onto Main Street to chase down the promises God gave me, and I've been tested since then more than anytime before.

I don't write this book looking back as a man who has arrived but as a man still running the race set before him. I fall, *a lot* ... but there is a Hand to help me get back up and run some more.

You may wonder where I am today. That's another story for another time, but I can tell you this. I have been tested *greatly* since the day I gave my life to Christ. As of this day I am struggling with my health, paying the price for the trials my body went through as a boy. At times it's been life or death. But a year from now I want this to be just another thing I have overcome.

And that's my point. It isn't you (or me) that gets us through. It's God, the One who is *stronger* than death and hell. The One who with one word spoke all of creation into existence. He is the footprints in the sand, the moments when we look back at the roughest times and see that it was Love who carried us through.

God has wired me a really stubborn man, and that's been part of the problem, especially when you have to learn to let go and let God take control. And then once you let go *of you*, you have to learn to hold on to something else—hope—and cling to that for dear life. That is all He asks us to do, *to be real*, by admitting that we can't do this life by ourselves. We need Him, and we need others. It's when we are real with God that God can be real with us.

As a man who has been there, I can vouch to that. I encourage you to do as I have and fix your eyes on the One who sits on High and hold fast. For when it is all said and done and we breath our last breath, I promise it's all going to make sense. The Son of Man is going to be standing before us, and we will have a life that will never end.

Hold onto hope, hold onto God for He will never fail us.

ACKNOWLEDGMENTS

My life has been a crazy ride, and I would not be here today if it weren't for countless people in my life who made it clear to me that they loved me.

But there have been others who made it their mission to see that I published my testimony. And I could not end this book without saying a formal thank-you to those folks:

- Rich Bullock. Rich, a lot of great men have come alongside me to help me become the man who was ready to tell my story. But I have never had a great man teach me and put in the work to help me tell my story. Thank you, man. Really. Thank you!

- Dylan McAfee and Tom Stephen. You guys have been the heart and soul behind the fire to tell my early life story. Thank you so very much!

- Nicole Merry. You are an excellent tutor! Show—don't tell. I will always remember that, written in gorgeous cursive, stroked in red ink! You were the first to roll up your sleeves and help me get this done. Thank you.

- Dan Balow. Dan, I have you to thank for so much. In the age of caller ID, you take my calls. You have always been in my corner with words of wisdom and genuine concern for me as a man, not as an author. Everyone I know today, I have met somehow through you and the respect you have garnished after many decades in the industry. Bless you, brother!

- Bruce Nygren. Bruce, you have been a champion for me and to me. I won't ever forget your belief in me and your wisdom and encouragement. You were one of the first in the industry to tell me that I should keep going until this happened. Thank you, Bruce!

- Cecil Murphey. I will never forget your generosity and your words of encouragement. And thank you for introducing me to your Minnesota friends!

- Steve Johnson. Brother, thank you. You helped connect me to the one person with the power to do something. I am so appreciative!

- David Sluka. I have only known you a short while, but I could tell the moment we met that you were a genuine man of integrity. Thank you for the mad hustle you have put in to turn this book around. I look forward to what lays ahead.

- Carlton Garborg. Carlton, thank you for believing in me and helping me. But moreso, thank you for being a brother. May the Lord continue to richly bless you, man!

- To John Franklin, Tom Stephen, Rich Bullock, Craig Johnson, Dr. Michael Stephen, Glen Garvin, Alan Smyth, Timothy Smith, Joshua Charles, Steve Sipp, and Sean Ellsworth—each one of you took hours out of your busy lives (lives of ministry and service to others) to read a rough manuscript. Each one of you have stood behind me and believed in me. Thank you all. And thanks to Tom Phillips from BGEA for reading my book during a busy Christmas season and providing your endorsement and encouragement.

- And to all the folks who read the pre-release and shared this story. Some of you have reached out to me to share your own story of encountering a love greater than all. Thank you. It has been your energy and passion that has propelled me farther. To dare to believe that a story of immense pain, redeemed by a fierce love, was worthy to tell. And tell loudly.

Thank you and God bless.

TO CONTACT THE AUTHOR

Please visit
MillennialOrphan.com

■ ■ ■

and follow Levi on Twitter
@levigideon

MillennialOrphan.com